MAENADS – EARLY DIONYSIAC RITES
Mihaela Jordanova

MAENADS –
EARLY DIONYSIAC RITES

Mihaela Jordanova

Sofia
2017

On the cover: Dionysos and his tiasos, fragment from Bororvo treasure.

ISBN 978-..................

CONTENTS

INTRODUCTION

The proposed presentation exposes a series of lectures devoted to the Thracian-Greek religious model of Dionysian festivity presented during seminars on ancient religion in Sofia and the New Bulgarian University. From ancient sources was reconstructed a cult reality associated with early forms of orgiastic mysticism and initial theoretical conclusions were drawn out about phenomenology of the problem. I focused on it due to the large interest that Bulgarian students from the humanities have shown to the problems of Thracian religion. Since the publication presents basic lectures, references to secondary criticism is detained at an absolute minimum. For the same reason the Ancient Greek texts are proposed in Latin transcription and an appendix is made with translations of some of the main sources.

In chapter one the traditional presuppositions about the *origins* of Dionysiac religion are examined, their bases in fact and argument are questioned and a new direction of enquiry is suggested. The tribal-gentilician roots of trieteric-orgiastic cult in Greece are discussed along with certain related issues such as the relation of gentilitial and divine names and epithets and the question of etymologies. A probable religio-gentilitial model is proposed: of a *royal clan*, who were in charge of the trieteric festival as a whole, and of a second clan, who were *carriers* of the *bacchica* and in charge specifically of the Bacchic initiations, with whom the *basileien genos* were bonded. Finally certain corollary assumptions of *invasion* theory, such as the god's putative beginnings among the lower orders of Greek society, are shown to be invalid on *a priori* grounds as well as erroneous *in fact*.

Naturally later tampering with the tribal-gentilician structures and general trends towards democratization at Athens and elsewhere, together with the concomitant growth and glamour of the dramatic festivals (including the importations of festival and cult belonging to alien *gene*, e.g. of Dionysos Eleuthereus at Athens) have all obscured the full ritual basis of this art and the *royal* gentilician-cultic structures in which it was embedded. In many of the most prominent cities the *royal clans* were in time far removed from the real centers of power, and Dionysiac offices devolved upon real but feeble *royalty* or upon the fictive counterparts of kings; accordingly, there would be increasingly detached and isolated *Bacchic branchs*. At the same time, however, the emergence of the Hellenistic kingdoms into the historical limelight on the peripheries of the Greek world reveals something in Dionysiac terms closer to the old patterns of divine and mortal relationships. For even through the veneer of rapid decadence generated in the hot-house airs of Alexandria and in the too luxurious vapours of Asia the Macedonian tribalistic roots are perspicuous: Ptolemaic kings and Pergamene princelings not only paid homage to the god prodigiously, but their cousins were his high priests and ministers and his rites and mysteries were their unquestioned *noble obligations*. Even at Athens there were vestiges of once proud combinations: of god and Medontid kings, of god and the wives of kings.

In chapter two we turn our attention to Thrace not in an attempt to *recover* the Urform of Dionysiac ritual but to trace the virtually identical form, organization and periodicity of the Thracian rites.

In the final chapters we come back to Greece to consider in order the continuity and universality of the *Trieterides* and the component phases of this long and complex festival (chapter three); and in chapter four we have a look at the festival's culminating phase, namely the *mixed feast* of masquerading men and women – the *Katagogia*. The festival structure and contours are outlined and the different character of its several feasts *segregated* and *mixed*, *private* and *public* phases are delineated. Maenadism, the restricted phase of the *baccheia gunaikon*, was but one phase of the *Trieterides*. The almost exclusive focus in the scholarship of this colourful biennieal phenomenon has obscured, even obliterated our comprehension of the trieteric-orgiastic rites as a whole and led to conclusions about historical change and development in the basic structure of the rites. The survey of the relevant source material is selective, not comprehensive.

CHAPTER I

THE PROBLEM OF *ORIGINS*

The question of *origins* has always bulked large in the study of Dionysiac religion; and it is right that it should continue to do so for perhaps some time. For apart from certain variations in views about *arrival* dates of the god and his particular *Heimatland* there is a remarkable uniformity of opinion among ancient authors and modern scholars alike concerning the cardinal tenet – the god's non-Greek origin and his un-Greek nature. For virtually all, he was an *invader*, his cult was *barbaronti*. The view put forward here is radically different – not merely different in degree:

- that the god was *echt* Greek as indeed he was Thracian and in all probability Lydian as well[1];
- that Dionysiac trieteric-orgiastic ritual and cult were embedded in the tribal-gentilician structures of the Greeks as they were in those of the Thracians; if one will speak of the *origin* of the god, one must speak of the origin of those Greek and Thracian tribes;
- that the categories *aristocratic* and *democratic* are for the most part completely inapposite given the complex nature of the rites and the character of the tribalistic societies of which they were a part;
- that Dionysos the god at all times and in all places *moved the best society*, and was at home in the Mycenaean places of kings as well as in the *Dark Age* shacks of the down-trodden and dispossessed: and if the accumulated *wisdom* of his cult – much of it passing under the name of *Orpheus* from the Archaic age – seemed to belong to a certain Bettelpriestermilieu,
- that same cult belonged *dia genous* to a number of tyrant princes of the age, some of whom, like the Peiststratids of Athens, traced their descent from the *basileia gene* of the Bronze Age.

In antiquity there was a diffusion of orgiastic Dionysiac religion, notably among Greeks, Macedonians, Thracians and Lydians. Yet we are in effect asked to believe one of two improbable propositions: either that the Greeks themselves were in *religious* terms *sui generis* and did not have kindred or comparable gods and practise similar rites – or that they had expurgated the *barbaric* elements in their own ritual practices, only to be reinfected by those very elements at a later time.

---

[1] See Фол, 1994, 63ff.

Myth does indeed suggest an *historical* transmission of an alien cult. And transmission is an unquestioned assumption of modern scholarship: given two or more sets of synchronic ritual *similia* an historical sequence of derivation is deduced from one putatively "original" set. This is pure *a priori* assumption. But we must realize too that a precondition of *invasion* theory is the completely untenable assumption of a ritual vacuum among the tribes and clans of Bronze Age Hellenes. For the Greeks indeed a ritual *tabula rasa* was a conceptual necessity: they could not conceive of an infinite regress of ritual precedents and practice into tribal time past. Furthermore it is reasonable to suppose that each tribe would be tenacious of its own rituals. We must therefore assume that at any given point on the time scale we are considering, i.e., from Greek historical times back into the *Urgrauenzeiten* of tribal time, each basic kinship unit, tribe, clan vel sim., would be as it were "ritually full". In cases of major culture change which was itself unmeasurably slow, ritual evolution would be slow, but most important, it would be internal: modification of *ta oikeia*, not adoption of *ta allotria*.

Myth represents a distinct type of evidence for the study of rituals. In the case of Dionysiac myth, however, matters are particularly confused; for there is no one straight methodological road to travel, and in addition to the Dionysiac *mythoi* proper there were other kinds of *logoi* which were in some fashion attached to Dionysiac cult. The so-called *introduction* or "resistance myths" not only reflect Dionysiac ritual but they were used in the rites themselves. Such myth was at once aetiological and paraenetic;[2] it was the property of priests and material for the poets, especially the tragic poets. There were moreover different kinds of Dionysiac myths which we may fairly assume will have reflected other phases of the highly complex festival of the god. These myths quite perspicuously reflect a segregated phase of the bacchic worship of men just as the *resistance* or *introduction myths*, at least in their main contours, reflect the segregated phase of the biennial worship of women which we normally designate by the term *maenadism*.

For the most part Dionysiac myths will have been the verbal corollaries of Dionysiac ritual. Whatever use was made of them in and by Dionysiac cult, it will not have altered in any significant sense their basic *shape*.[3] The Greek

---

[2] See Фол, 1994, 8ff. For a general discussion of this category of myth see Kirk, 1970, 254ff. These Dionysiac myths belong to group two in Kirk's suggested typology of functions which he calls "operative, iterative and valedictory"; his primary example is from Near Eastern mythology, and he makes no mention of Dionysiac myth or ritual in this context. Theokr. 26 is a good example of this type, its difficulties notwithstanding; see 58f. The poem is a rather unusual conflation of myth and non-mythologized ritual detail.

[3] But their inherent cynicism led the Greeks on occasion a least to suspect foul play; see. e.g. Diod. I 23.6 which indicates that the Greeks themselves were well aware of the

myths in general provided the poets with an unending and diverse stock of *paradeigmata*, and Dionysiac myth in particular provided both secular poet and cult with explicit and ominous inducements to correct action vis-à-vis the god(s): *to fight against god* (*theomahein*) was to invite divine reprisals, the vengeance of the son of Zeus, Dionysos, or of Zeus himself. The important thing is to bear in mind the essential distinction between the primary form of *resistance myth* and its secondary function:[4] its function will not have determined its particular form. Dionysiac *theology*, in contradiction to Dionysiac myth, was the product of the manifestly self-conscious search for the meaning of the objects and acts of Dionysiac cult – its symbols – and for a *true account* of the nature of its god.[5] We in turn in our search for the *origins* of Dionysiac religion would do well to look beyond the many and diverse kinds of *logoi* which had accreted round its rituals, and to beware especially of those which seem to have an *historical* plausibility.

All myth is in some sense composite, and resists overly facile categorisation. But certain categories, e.g., aetiological, do have at least a logical validity: the same feature in a given myth, e.g., the *invasion* of the god in Dionysiac cult – myth, cannot be two (methodologically) opposed things at the same time. It cannot be both aetiological and historical. It is, however, just here that we encounter a pronounced methodological ambivalence in the scholarship. For the majority of scholars who speak about the so-called resistance myths on the one hand profess, that they are indeed aetiological, yet on the other proceed quite inexplicably to use them as historical evidence for the putative *invasion* of a foreign cult and the *resistance* of the *invaded* people. Guthrie, for example, explicitly cautions against accepting these myths as straight history because he believes them to be aetiological. But once the warning has been issued, he goes on to adopt what can only be called a full-fledged historical interpretation of the myths on the basis of what he decided is their *core of historical fact*.[6] Dodds too seems somewhat ambivalent about these matters:

> *Unlike most Greek tragedies the Bacchae is a play about an historical event – the introduction into Hellas of a new religion. When Eurpidies wrote the event lay in the far past, and the memory of it survived only in mythical forms; the new religion has long since been acclimatized and accepted as part of Greek life; … the forces liberated and embodied by the original movement were active in other forms in the Athens of Euripides' day.*[5]

myth-ritual correlation.

[1] See Marazov, 2000, 30ff.

[5] See Dodds, 1960, XXVI.

There can be few scholars who would maintain openly that myth provides legitimate evidence for the study of the history of the very matter of which it treats – in this case the history of Dionysiac cult. This would of course be tantamount to claiming that the *invasion*, the *first time*, into which the mythopoetic processes turn the regular, repeated and real *gignomena* of ritual is in fact one *mutatis mutandis* with the hypothetical *hapax genomenon* of history, in this case the arrival of a foreign cult and the ensuing resistance and eventual submission of the Greeks. But methodological inconsistency is tolerated, and exactly this result is achieved. We even find this same historical interpretation of cult-myth in G.S. Kirk's study of Greek myths – a context where we might least expect to find it:

> *Finally Dionysos, the god who came down into Greece through Thrace, ultimately from Phrygia in Asia Minor, and became the focus of an ecstatic religion… Some interpreters have been tempted to take these (sc. The cult-myths) as reflections of actual historical resistance to his cult (which reached Greece comparatively late, perhaps after 1000 B.C.), and that could be so. The myth of Pentheus at Thebes, after all, depicts a whole city at odds with the god in various ways. But there is also an individual, psychological level of meaning. Dionysus represents the irrational element in man, and his myths the conflict between reason and social convention on the one side, emotion on the other.*[8]

Kirk too then equivocates; but for him aetiology does not seem to come in at all; Dionysiac myth is a mixture of *history* and *psychology*. It seems at this point entirely fair to say that at regards the interpretation of *introduction myth* we are caught in a *vicious circle*; for interpretation is inexplicably bound up with the scholarly preconceptions about the nature and *origins* of Dionysiac religion, and is guided almost exclusively by them. Given these preconceptions Dionysiac myth will invariably meet the test of apparent plausibility. But whatever our views of Dionysiac *Herkunft*, we must be aware of methodological pitfalls, and take especial care to avoid this particular error. The cult-mythical *invasion* of the god may not be used as corroborative evidence for a theory which postulates the *arrival* of a foreign cult (at whatever period) and the *resistance* of the Greeks. Certainly it cannot provide the basis for such a theory.

We have seen that the Dionysiac *invasion per se* is a mythological construct devoid of any historical validity of its own. But the specific *Herkunft* which Greek myth assigned to the god is a matter which still poses problems. For if *invasion* belongs properly to ritual, i.e. is strictly aetiological, the very specificity of divine nationality does not. As presented for example in the *Bacchae* it seems indeed to belong not to the primary mythopoetic structure but to a layer of secondary elaboration. The former had left a significant gap to be filled in: the *whither* of the divine *invasion* of course will have been fixed in accordance with the locus of cult at the time of the formulation of its myth;[6] the *whence* we must assume was not similarly fixed, but will have been answered by some process that we should equate, however roughly, with *historia*. It is most unfortunate that we know both the whither and whence of the divine *invasion* only in the case of the Theban cult of the god.[7]

Before examining some of the particular *semeia* and *tekmeria* which might have induced the Greeks to think of the land they usually called Lydia as the *original* home of the god, and to incorporate the view into their Dionysiac myth-history, we will briefly consider another form of Dionysiac myth with which *introduction myth* is manifestly correlated. For it is the quite explicit Lydian *Herkunftsgeschichte* of the *Bacchae* that leads us plausibly to assume that the myth of this invading god is inextricably bound up with a specifically Lydian version of the so-called myth of the Double Birth, i.e., of a second, divine, birth from the father of the god in the Tmolos mountains. Whether or not Euripides intentionally suppressed the exact location of the second birth, we cannot know; he does, however, refer twice to its occurrence;[8] but we can be reasonably certain that in the version Euripides was following, Zeus will have gone to Lydian Tmolos *to be accomplished*.[9] Conversely, the 49th Orphic Hymn, which speaks explicitly of the Tmolos range as the place where Zeus went to bear his son, does not mention the first, *birth*.[10] Theban *resistance myth* was then in all likelihood co-ordinated with Lydian *second birth myth*; but they were also plainly detachable.

The diffusion of second births is of some interest as is the range of nationalities represented: Libya, Aithiopia, Phoincia, Lydia, Bithynia.[11] Apparently in an earlier age there was some variation also in the accounts of the first birth;

---

[6] The transition from cult-myth to *religious* or dogmatic myth (namely, the myth attached to, specifically, the Theban cult of the god which in time attained to a kind of universal validity for virtually all Dionysiac cults whatever their local-gentile bases) is a development too complex to consider here. Interesting, however, in this connexion is Diod. I 23, 6. The First Homeric Hymn shows plainly that at an earlier period there were still in existence alternatives to the Theban "first birth" from Semele, and the controversy, it would seem, was still quite lively.

[7] Eur. Ba. 13; see Dodds ad loc., and 23.

[8] Ba. 88-98 and 523ff; cf. the ironic querie at ib. 467.

[9] Ib. 463.

[10] cf. Hymn Orph. 49, to Hipta, nurse of Bacchos and Steph. Byz. s.v. Mastaura.

[11] Hdt. 2.146 purports to represent the 5th C communis opinio, and recalls the rather adamant view of the author of the Hymn Hom. I; see below n. 19. Cf. Arrian (F.H.G. 3.592) who locates the birth far to the north in Bithynia, and cf. Eustath. ad Dion. 939.

the places, however, are all Greek.[12] But in time by virtually common consent of the Greeks the birth from Semele was said to have taken place in Boeotian Thebes. Other cities to keep up Dionysiac appearances could claim some specially sacred spot. Most, however, if they made a claim at all, pointed to a local *wine miracle* to mark the epiphany of their Dionysos. Whether by say classical times Lydia had become the divine *Heimatland* par excellence in Greek Dionysiac myth in much the same way that Thebes had become the place of the first, mortal, birth *ex virgine* is something we cannot know. Its correlation with Theban *Dionysiaka*, however, would conceivably have encouraged that development. It is moreover a reasonable assumption that each major myth-making centre, e.g. Tiryns, Boeotian Orchomenos etc., will have had at one time a specific (for the most part) foreign place of the second birth with which the Dionysiac *invasion* on their own territory was correlated. For the question *whence* will have been in each case equally relevant. We may therefore quite plausibly deduce from the various known (and uncorrelated) places of the divine second birth some of the different points of origin for a number of mythical *invasions*. It is useless to try to speculate about which may have been correlated with which. What we can say in very general terms is that the mother-son relationship seems to belong to Greece proper while the birth from the father belongs principally to foreign places in the East.

The origin and significance of the myth of the double birth remain an unsolved puzzle. Comparisons, e.g. with the Vedic god Soma and his residence in the right thigh of the supreme *sky-god* Indra are of course of interest; and there are other more far-away parallels of birth from the thigh.[13] Too often, however, such parallels deflect our attention away from what might be more pressing questions. It is in fact the overall structure of the myth which must concern us here: premature birth disappearance/gestation and rebirth. In brief the myth allows for two things. First, as we have seen, it accommodates *introduction myth*: it gets the Greek-born son of Semele out of Greece and gives him a *foreign* birth and citizenship at least where we find it correlated with the first Greek birth as at Thebes. It thus allows for the *invasion* of a properly *foreign* god, and as such it appears to be in mythopoetic terms a necessary adjustment to the primary (aetiological) layer of cult-myth. The second point concerns the relation of birth myth (first and second) to ritual epiphany. It is quite natural that the day of the epiphany of a god at a particular festival would be explained in terms of the first appearance of the god, namely, the day of his birth. Statius explicitly connects the myth of the Theban birth with the ritual epiphany of the god at Thebes which in his account is accompanied by a *wine miracle*. It is in

---

[12] Theokr. 26.33, Eustath. Ad Il. 18.486 and Diod. 3.68ff.
[13] See Marazov, 2000, 20ff.

fact relatively straightforward to correlate the ritual epiphany of the god with the first mortal birth *ex virgine*. Again, in the 44th *Orphic Hymn* the connexion is made quite explicit.[14]

There is very little difficulty then in correlating the first birth with the ritual epiphany of the god at his biennial festival, the *Trieterides*. What, however, are we now to make of the second birth? To be truly consistent we must expect a ritual correlate of some kind for it as well. As we shall see below, in some detail the *trieteric days*, which were given over to the celebration of Dionysos Baccheios will have included a variety of rites, and the festival complex as a whole will have been marked by discrete phases. Some ritual activities were segregated, some called for mixed participation of men and women. We know that in some sense the god will have appeared to the women in private, i.e. to the *baccheia gunaikon*.[15] But *bacchic* men also secured an *epiphany* of the god at their *baccheia*. A Rhodian inscription from the time of the emperor Caracalla mentions explicitly an *awakening* of the god.[16] The same inscription also seems to resolve our major difficulty, namely, the two correlated epiphanies which we deduce from the myth of the double birth; for it speaks of the two descents of the god before breaking off.[17] And indeed the idea of two epiphanies is quite out of the question should we be unable to establish the fact that there was at some point, following the first and prior to the second epiphany, a ritual *disappearance*. Conversely, the two *disappearances* of the inscription are inexplicable apart from the two *appearances*. The Rhodian inscription thus confirms the suspected myth-ritual correlation: premature birth – transference / gestation-rebirth equals (nebulous), epiphany-disappearance – return. Where do we have a festival of the *Return* attested by its very name, namely, for the Attic-Ionian cities, we lack the specific information which the Rhodian inscription supplies about a second disappearance.

In Greek myth some centrifugal force sent the father of the god to the four corners of the known world to bear his *insown* son. And from these distant quarters the god was imagined to *return* every second year when he made his second and fully *mature* epiphany. Diodorus twice seems to allude to the Ionian *Feast of the Return* – the *Katagogia* – setting it within the context of the Hellenistic favourite, the mythical return of the god from the conquered Indians. The Eastern conquest, in particular the India campaign, remained

---

[14] See Sources application

[15] See e.g. Diod. 4.3; Plut. de Is et Os 365;

[16] Bakheia hois tō …epegeironti ton theon. Nilsson rightly connects this inscription with another belonging to the Hellenistic age which attests the trieteric periodicity of the Rhodian baccheia (male). See Nilsson, 1957 (hereafter referred to as DM) 64.

[17] …kai tois theou de kathodois dysi ton…

throughout later antiquity the most plausible *myth-historical* explanation for the biennial Dionysiac fests: the loot became the *spoils* of a *war* waged by the motley crew of *daimones* in the entourage of the god, who *returned* and revealed himself every second year, to set the cities of Greece dancing in his honour. All this the Greeks understood as commemorative performance, celebrating the hypothetical "first time" of their trieteric ritual.[18]

As we shall see below, the events of the earlier part of the *Trieterides* were not forgotten: the Bacchoi and the Bacchai had a prominent role in the ceremonies of the *Return* as did those winsome, hirsute, comrades of the god, the satyrs.[19] In the parodos of the *Bacchae* Euripides makes explicit reference to the *Trieterides* and to the role of the satyrs at these festivals;[20] like Diodoros, he too seems to allude to the Attic-Ionian feast, called the *Katagogia* setting it within the context of a *return* from the East, in this case the *bringing home* of the god from the Phrygian mountains – one of the places, we will recall, of the divine birth from the thigh. The following antistrophe in fact relates the myth of the double birth without designating the place of the paternal birth.

Among the Dionysiac discussions of late antiquity we find a suggested correlation between the first birth from Semele and the first round of biennial orgiastic activity, which was, like the premature birth itself, incomplete. The same author goes on to correlate by implication the divine conquest of India and the second and final round of orgiastic activity, which will have constituted the culmination of the *trieterides hemerai*, during which the god made his second and full-fledged epiphany.[21] We in turn quite plausibly deduce the connexion, in the emperor Julian's mind, between these two sets of orgiastic ritual.

The ritual pattern of trieteric epiphanies (appearance – disappearance – return) then required, and was matched by a myth which told of a first and of a second birth. And the logic of Dionysiac cult-mythical aetiology itself demanded a foreign citizenship, and therefore a foreign birth, for the *invading* god. Neither the departure of the father of the god to bear his son nor the return of the *thighborn* god to the land of his first birth have anything to do with a real historical event – the hypothetical *introduction* into Greece of a new religion. Neither are *survivals* in *folk memory*. The specificity of the *Herkunft* on the other hand which Dionysiac myth-history assigns to the god is a matter worthy of consideration. For at the level of secondary elaboration there is no reason why myth would not seek an historical plausibility. The Lydian nationality of the god which is specified in the one fairly complete surviving piece of

---

[18] See Eur. Ba. 21f.
[19] See Diod. 4.3; Himer. Or. XIV 26.
[20] See Василева, 22ff.
[21] Ex Indōn ho Dionysos autoptos efaineto.

Dionysiac myth-history may well have a validity comparable to that of any other conclusion reached by ancient *historia*: it will have been a deduction made on the basis of certain available *semeia* and tekmeria.

The major contenders for the title of divine *Heimatland* today are Asia Minor and Thrace.[22] In antiquity the picture was a little bit more complex: Egyptian *Herkunft* was a subject of scholarly discussion at least as early as the Archaic age. Thrace, the favourite of modern scholarship, was known to the Greeks as perhaps the Dionysiac territory *par excellence*, but they did not think of their own Dionysiac ritual as *derived* from their northern neighbours.[23] Neither in their myth nor in their scholarly speculations was their adoptive god – as they saw him – a Thracian *stranger*. On the contrary, their own myths told of a Dionysiac *invasion* of Thrace too and of the *resistance* of a Thracian king.

Among scholars it is Nilsson, pre-eminently, who devised a theory of Dionysiac *origins* comprehensive enough to accommodate both a Thracian and a Lydian god. According to this bi-partite view the got had not one, but two, *houses*, and from each of these he had come on different occasions. That some ultimate connection could be found between these two Dionysi is of less significance than the fact that the two were, by the time of their respective arrivals on Greek soil, of different natures, and were accordingly celebrated by different sorts of rites. The Thracian god had retained his *original* character, while the Lydian (Phrygian) god had been *contaminated*, even transmogrified, by indigenous.[24] Both Dodds and Guthrie seem in some sense to accept this view – Dodds finding probable verification in the myths which *suggest* that the god may have arrived by two independent routes, Guthrie, in the putatively *original* Phrygian home of the mother of the god Semele.[25] Nilsson's subsequent modifications of his view of Lydian Bacchos seem not to have deterred scholars from finding this view of bi-partite *origins* inherently plausible. Nilsson in the end had rejected strictly on seasonal grounds his former equation of the Dionysos Liknites of Delphi with the Lydian Dionysos who, according to Himerios, was awakened in the spring of the year.[26] But we might reconsider briefly Nilsson's basic proposition; for it is the methodology itself that must be questioned. According to Nilsson it was the god of the trieteric orgia, of maenads and of omophagy, who had come from Thrace. This bearded northerner bore little resemblance in any of his outward manifestations to Lydian Bacchos. The latter was a child, the*child in the*

---

[22] See Фол, 1994, 68ff.

[23] Those Greeks who were not proponents of the theory which derived virtually all *sophia* from Egypt may well have thought of Dionysiac *theology* as having a Thracian *origin*.

[24] See MMR 2, 492ff. and 567ff.

[25] See Dodds, Ba. xxi and Guthrie, op. cit. 154.

[26] GGR 3, I 580.

liknon, who was born, and died, annually. He was in other words a *vegetation* god. Nilsson had built his theory upon one rather slight notice in the late Bithynian born rhetorician, Himerios.[27]

The Greek is admittedly somewhat ambiguous; for on the one hand we know that the *mad revels* – the orgiastic rites of the god – were a biennial phenomenon, and that this bienniality, since it was in fact synonomous with the orgia, will have been more often than not simply taken for granted when the Greaks talked about them. On the other hand, the different season of the Lydian orgia might well cause us to question whether we are not in fact dealing with fundamentally different rites and therefore, possibly annual ones – if indeed we regard the season itself as a point of critical importance. There is no doubt that the biennial orgia took place in winter (Lenaion) in the Ionian states; and it is quite likely that at Megara and in her colonies, e.g. Herakleia, (Kallatis) and Astakos, they took place in the same month – the Megarian-Bithynian month of Dionysos. Certainly they were a winter phenomenon at Delphi – and probably in most places: Ovid (F. I 393f.) obviously thought of them as occurring universally in winter. But if Agrionios was in fact a spring month in Boeotia, then Thebes and Lydia will have celebrated the orgia in same season. This is of course of interest in terms of the myth-historical *Herkunft*.

But the very verbs Himerios uses suggest a similar set of rites in honour of the same god. It was the supposed annual periodicity and the season which led Nilsson to assum, that this Dionysos was a *vegetation god* in contradiction to Dionysos Thrax, the god of the *maenads*, who returned only every second year and, as is generally agreed, in the winter. What information we have had all along about Dionysos Liknites rather suggests that he is none other than the god who, according to Nilsson's schematic division, had come from Thrace. For we know that this Liknites was *awakened* by the Thyiads of Delphi who were the women who *raved* every second year *in the mountains* when the god made his epiphany.[28] The Lydian Liknites was a scholarly construct of the *analytical* method: the hypothetical *vegetation god* whose pattern of appearance and disappearance is by definition annual is out of joint at Delphi where the biennial orgia of the nominally same god are well attested.[29] But apparently disparate elements and discrepancies can be accounted for in historical terms: they are accretions, different elements coming from different places at different times. The whole is thus an analysable sum of different parts. The *syncretism*

---

[27] Lydoi men oun… tō Dionysō bakheuontes… mainontas men tō theō kai horeuousin, epeidan autois ear enenke tas hōras ameiban ho helios… Lydois mrn oun ear Dionysos agei kai ta Dionysou bakheumata…

[28] Plut. De Is. (364D-365A).

[29] Paus. 10.32.5.

here, however, is in the scholarship, it is not demonstrably in the Dionysiac ritual of Delphi.[30] Nilsson himself eventually saw that a Lydian Bacchos was not an aid to the scholarly clarity of the Dionysiac situation at Delphi, and he rejected him. But he retained to the end his bi-partite view of Dionysiac *origins* and of two escentially different Dionysi, one Thracian god and one Lydo-Phrygian.[31]

No plausible theory of *origins* of course is possible in the first place without the existence of certain signs that point to a given place of the hypothetical Herkunft or without certain evidence that indicates the practice of nominally or structurally similar rites in that place. In the case of Lydia we are moderately well supplied with various kinds of indicators as well as with explicit evidence attesting the practice of orgiastic Dionysiac religion in that land. We will briefly review some of these, and consider in turn what deductions we may legitimately make on the basis of them. We have considered in passing above how myth itself is a kind of indicator of Lydian ritual: the Lydian specificity of the divine citizenship in the Bacchae for example is indirect evidence for Greek awareness of Dionysiac rites of an orgiastic nature in the valleys of the Tmolos mountains at least as early as the date of the composition of the play and probably much earlier. Fragments of specifically Lydian second birth myth such as we find in the 48th*Orphic Hymn* point in the same direction.[32] There is an alternative version of the *invasion* of Thebes by a Lydian *stranger* preserved by the Roman poet Ovid, in which the *stranger* is a mortal man – Tyrrhenus Acoetus.[33]

We have noted the reference of Himerios to the Lydian rites of Dionysos Bacchos in his own day; this testimony is admittedly rather late. But already in

---

[30] In his last major work Nilsson was concerned not so much with the issue of the specific country of *origin* of Liknites as with his apparently "chthonian" nature, DM 38-45. The child in the liknon, who according to the original view, was the symbol of the annual rebirth of vegetation in the spring, is here a very different child. He is related to the *child Dionysos* who was dismembered by the Titans. Thus is effected a union of the once Lydian, annual, *vegetation god* and the *Orphic*, chthonian, trieteric god who is also apparently a child. And the bearded (and biennial) Thracian is left unaccounted for while the *nurses* of the child (ritual maenadism) have been tacitly relegated.

[31] GGR 3, I 580f. … sie (sc. die Vegetationsriten) verbinden sich viel natürlicher mit dem lydisch-phrygisch als mit dem thrakischen Dionysos.

[32] Cf. nr. 49 to Hipta, 1.6; Nonn. D. 40.273; Kern, OF, fr.199.

[33] Met. III 576ff. Cf. Hymn Hom. 7; Clem. Al. Protr. 2.16. We cannot consider here the vexed, but obviously germane, question of Lydian-Etruscan connexions. But we can note in passing that there is a relative abundance of archaeological evidence from the Archaic period on which attest Dionysiac religion in Etruria. Also of considerable importance is Livy's testimony that it was an ignoble Greek from Etruria who was responsible for the introduction of Bacchic rites at Rome in the early 2nd C B.C.: sacrificulus et vates, occultorum et nocturnorum antistes sacrorum…, 39. 8; on which see Nilsson, DM, 14ff.

the *Bacchae* we have evidence which attests the contemporary practice of Dionysiac rites in Lydia. The *parodos(135ff)* describes the traditional *eis oros* of trieteric Dionysiac ritual without any mythical colouring whatsoever.[34] The mountains are those of Lydia-Phrygia. He is sweet in the mountains, whenever after the running dance he falls on the ground, wearing the sacred garment of fawn skin, hunting the blood of the slain goat, a raw-eaten delight, rushing to the [140] *Phrygian, the Lydian mountains, and the leader of the dance is Bromius, evoe!* The plain flows with milk, it flows with wine, it flows with the nectar of bees. The Bacchic one, raising the flaming torch of pine on his thyrsos, like the smoke of Syrian incense, darts about, arousing the wanderers with his racing and dancing,

The special Dionysiac vestments, the sacramental meal of *raw flesh*, the ritual use of milk, wine, honey and incense, belonged no less to the bacchic rites of the Lydians than they did to those of the Greeks – if we are to believe Euripides. And we have little reason not to. Both Lydians and Greeks then will have gone *to the mountains* to revel and celebrate their god. Perhaps the most tangible indication of a Lydian-Dionysiac connexion is the god's very name: *Bacchos*, the name (in both upper and lower case) that the god shared with his own votaries, is said to have been of Lydian origin.[35] The claim is a serious one. For Bacchos was alternative name of the god in a way that his other epithets were not. This *second name* and its derivatives, Baccheios, Bacchios, etc. were to be found virtually throughout the Greek world; most important, they were to be found among the three major tribal divisions of the Greeks: in the Milesian colony of Olbia on the northern shores of the Euxine from the time of her foundation, c. 645 B.C., men will have been initiated into the rites of *Dionysos Baccheios*.[36] From this information we easily deduce the generalised practice of *bacchikai teletai* in honour of Dionysos Baccheios among the Ionian populations of Asia Minor during the Archaic period. Again from Megarian Herakleia's (Pontic) colony, Kallatis, is deduced the trieteric "bacchic" worship of Dionysos in Dorian Megara at least as early as the 7th/6th century B.C. And finally, we have direct evidence which attests the worship of Dionysos *Bucchis* among the Aeolic speaking people of Lesbos during the same period. We may therefore safely conclude that the rites of Dionysos Bacchos were not only established in the city-states of Archaic Greece, but that they were a part of the *establishment religion* in those states.

---

[34] See Seaford, 1981, 252-275, Versnel, 134-135.
[35] See e.g. Nilsson, GGR 3, I 581 "Der andere Name des Gottes, Bakchos, ist lydischen Ursprunges"; cf. id. "Bakchos cin lydisches Wort ist"; Dodds, 1953, xx.
[36] See e.g. Hdt. 4.79 and 108

A bilingual inscription from Sardis which belongs to the 4th century B.C., renders the Lydian *bakiwali* as the Greek Dionysikles.[37] For some scholars this stone has provided concrete and unimpeachable evidence of the Lydian origin of the name Bacchos and, simultaneously, confirmation of the theory of the Lydian origin of the bacchic rites themselves. But even if we accept that Baki (=Bacchos) is the Lydian name for Dionysos, it does not follow necessarily that the name came to Greek from Lydian.[38] There is, however, general agreement that the name Bacchos is not Greek.[39] If, therefore, we reject the assumption that the name is of Lydian origin, we seem nevertheless reduced to speculation about other possible foreign sources.

The serious alternative seems to be the hypothetical Semitic origin of the world. A Semitic, and specifically Phoinician, etymology was in fact known in antiquity.[40] Indeed the idea of the Phoinician *Herkunft* must have seemed to the Greeks of very early times to have had a certain *historical* plausibility; for we find woven into the fabric of Dionysiac myth-history certain specifically Phoinician strands, which the historian Herodotos endeavoured to raise to the level of *historia*. But while scholars from other disciplines have not been shy to take up the case for the Semitic *background* of the *Bacchic* ritual of the Greeks, it is fair to say, that classical scholars for the most part have been loath to give it serious consideration. However, the case has been reopened by W. Burkert:

> *"Bacchos" könnte auch ein semitisches Lehnwort in der Bedeutung "Weinen" sein, wobei die Griechinnen, die Dionysossuchen, den Frauen Is-raels, die, "den Tammuz beweinen" entsprechen würden. Dass ältere*

---

[37] See E. Littman, Sardis VI 1, 1916 38f = Friedrich nr. 116; cf. nr. 22, 9; R. Gusmani, 1964, s.v. bakilli-, bakivali. The Sprachverwandtschaft is still an unsolved puzzle: Lydian was once thought to be related to Etruscan. Nilsson's expressed certainty thatit was not Indo-european (GGR 3 I 581) was overly optimistic.

[38] Cf. e.g. W. Burkert, 1985, 253 "Dass Semele ein thrakisch-phrygisches Wort für "Erde" ist, lässt sich freilich so wenig sichern wie die Priorität von lydisch baki- gegenüber Bacchos als Name des Dionysos". Cf. West, 1978, 373f. I cannot agree that Dion. is the male counterpart of a tree nymph nor that Dion.'s votaries "impersonate the tree nymphs who reared him" when they carry the fennel wands. As for West's views on the name Bacchos itself, it must suffice here to say that bakchos=klados surely has more to do with the nature of poetic diction – a case of transferred epithet – than with etyma and/or ritual.

[39] E.g. W. Burkert, 1985, 253. "Mit Nichtgriechischem ist zweifellos zu rechnen Semele als Mutter, Bacchos als Name des Verehrers und Zweitname des Thyrsos als sein heiliger Stab..."

[40] Hesych. s.v. bakchon.

kilikisch-syrische Beziehungen durch spätere phrygische, dann lydische überlagert wurden, ist durchaus möglich.[41]

The chain of transmission which Burkert has outlined, even if entirely plausible, must remain within the realm of pure speculation. But such hypotheses are the inevitable consequence of the assumption of the *un-Greekness* of the name Bacchos. It would be well, however, to look rather more closely at this basic assumption. For we are indeed confronted with a proposition that is anomalous in religious-historical terms and one that is improbable in onomastic terms: On the one hand we have the god Dionysos; about the Minoan-Mycenaean *Herkunft* of his name and of at least certain aspects of his cult there is now virtual certainty. On the other hand we have the god (Dionysos) Bacchos: about the non-Greek *Herkunft* of his name there is general scholarly agreement. In the event, however, apart from a priori assumptions about what does and does not constitute *to Hellenikon*, it is the name alone that leads scholars to assume the foreign origin of his cult. The full implication of this view is that there must have been an accretion of *bacchic* elements round the older Dionysiac rites of the Greeks of the Bronze Age. This means of course that the specifically bacchic aspects of Dionysiac cult, ritual and nomenclature, which we are wont to think of as the quintessentially *Dionysisac*, will have been lacking in the cult of the Mycenaean Dionysos.

First we might consider the question of when this hypothetical development could have taken place. Our evidence shows plainly that the bacchic form of Dionysiac religion was diffused over much of the Greek world by the Archaic period. Some scholars, however, take it as axiomatic that the Dorian *genos* of the Bacchi(a)dai was called eponymously after the god Dionysos Bacchos; accordingly, we can obtain a *terminus ante quem* sometime round the middle of the *Dark Age* for the hypothetical assimilation by the Dorian Greeks of the putatively foreign *bacchica*. But since it is generally taken for granted that the cult-myths reflect a *bacchic* form of Dionysiac worship, and further, that they have a Mycenaen origin, we plausibly deduce the Mycenaean practice of an essentially similar type of rites to those which are well attested for the Archaic and classical periods and which are denominated *bacchic*. Herodotos himself corroborates these deductions when he links a Pylian (therefore by definition, Bronze Age) Melampous with this form of Dionysiac worship.[72] The association of the god Dionysos, albeit without the explicit *bacchic* designation, with Neleid Pylos is in fact confirmed by the Pylos tablets as is the presence at Pylos of the *genos* of the Melampodidai. Therefore as far back as we can trace the Mycenaean Dionysos we may quite legitimately deduce the *bacchic*

---

[41] Burkert, ibidem.

nature of at least some of his rites. It is moreover only reasonable to assume that there will have been an onomastic as well as a ritual continuity, i.e., if there were Bronze Age rites of the orgiastic or *bacchic* kind performed in honour of the Mycenaean Dionysos, they will have been *bacchic* in name as well as in form.[42] Accordingly, we have not only a virtually certain *Dark Age* date – c. 10th century B.C. at the latest – for the presence of *onomata bacchica* in Greece but a probable Bronze Age one. It follows that any incursions of a foreign *bacchic* cult and subsequent onomastic *contaminatio* of an ultimately Semitic origin will have to have occurred at a very early period indeed.

But before we turn our attention to the question of divine and gentile names and of their transferability, we might briefly consider the question of adoption – in this case of the wholesale adoption of a complex of alien sacrificial ritual by tribes of Greeks who will have performed their own rituals (and presumably held their own *beliefs*). The traditional view held by perhaps the majority of modern scholars and fostered in the first instance by the cult-myths themselves is the *hysteria*-contagion theory: there was an *invasion* of a foreign cult whose members were so militant and/or whose rituals were so infectious that the initial resistance of the indigenous population was overcome. The rather more dignified theory of a *doctrinal* conversion and the concomitant adoption of the ritual bases of that *doctrine* is after all but a slight modification of the former. Both entail certain questionable presuppositions about the nature of ritual and about the character of tribalistic society.

There are, however, several *a priori* arguments against the assumption which holds effectively that one set of foreign *bacchic* Dionysiac rites were adopted by a people who practised either another set of *non-bacchic* Dionysiac rites or merely other rites. By a series of plausible inferences we have placed the Dionysiac *bacchica* squarely within the *religious* activities of the aristocratic *gene* of Bronze Age Greece. But we cannot on the basis of those same inferences state categorically, that the bacchic rites were either indigenous to Greece, or that they were embedded in the tribal structures of the Greeks whatever the ultimate *origin* of the Greek tribes. At this point, however, we may gain some clarity if we reflect briefly upon the nature of tribalism. For in the religious life of any given community tribalism implies a very high degree of conservatism – a rigid tenaciousness of *ta oikeia*, both rituals and names, and an imperviousness to *ta kaina*.[43] And there can be little doubt of the applicability of the

---

[42] For a summary see Dimitrov, 2012, 23ff.

[43] There is a passage from Plato's *Laws* , which is germane to this issue, because it is often quoted in misleading contexts. When Plato imposes severe penalties on *any person who practices orgiastic rites other than the public ones*, he is legislating against *ta nomisthenta*: the orgia were ta *kata ta patria*. These are not the orgia of *xenikoi theoi*

term to Greek society during the period we are considering; for the politically and intellectually sophisticated society of the Greek city-states showed pronounced traces of tribalism, most conspicuously in the religious sphere, even well into the classical period and beyond.

There is a related point. If we cannot speak with certainty of the embeddedness of specifically bacchic ritual in Hellenic tribal structures, we may nevertheless legitimately speak of the tribal embeddedness of sacrificial rituals in general. This means that certain patterns of sacrifice will have been scrupulously preserved within fixed racial or kinship units, and adhered to by being passed down from one generation to the next.[44] Thus we may argue that this very conservatism both in the matter of the form of ritual sacrifice and of the *traditional* preservation of that form within and by the members of a restricted kinship group – family, clan or tribe – speaks against the assumption of the transferability of sacrificial rituals in societies, that can be classified as tribalistic in some degree. Furthermore, we know that at the heart of the bacchic rites lay the act of sacrifice, or, more a series of sacrificial acts which formed a pattern so complex that we have yet to apprehend it in its entirety.

Finally it seems categorically wrong to assume that one type of sacrificial ritual, for example, is *originally* native to one people and foreign to another and in turn to account for the two separate sets of attested or inferred ritual *similia* by positing an historical relationship between the two, i.e., one of *origin* and *derivation*. The same arguments against the transferability of sacrificial rituals apply to the hypothetical transmission and adoption of foreign names. Indeed it seems fair to say that the adoption of *xenica onomata* apart from the ritual (-doctrinal) complex to which they properly belong is an even less persuasive proposition. There is, however, an additional, historical point: If the theory of the transmission of names and/or rituals has been shown to be questionable on *a priori* grounds, the chronology of the possible sequence of transmission

---

(see e.g. Dodds, xxiv): we may well suspect that it was just here that we should look for the *origins* of theurgic practices. The contrast in the Platonic text is between such *private* and unsanctioned acts and effects and between ones that are publicly sanctioned, and not between *public* and *foreign*. The techniques are *oikeia* but *para kairon*.

[44] The example of the Eumolpidai at Eleusis is too well knows to require comment. The question of the possible connexions of the *genos* of the Melampodidai with Dionysiac sacrificial in historical terms is far too complex to try to assess here. It is arguable, however, that Herodotos, will have had some sort of contemporary evidence for his gentilitial deductions (for this is what they are: a Melampous will have been a member of that *genos* which continued in parts of the Greek world onomastically intact well into Classical times) at 2.49; cf. Paus. I 43.5. Teiresias and the Melampodidai meet once again at Kolophon.

suggested by Burkert also appears somewhat doubtful in light of both our certain and of our probable dates for Dionysiac *bacchica* in mainland Greece.

But if for the reasons we have discussed the adoption of a foreign ritual-doctrinal complex by the Greeks of the *Dark Age*, or earlier, seems an untenable proposition, we are nevertheless left with the problem posed by the apparently foreign name which is most certainly attached to that complex. So we seem after all to be back at the point where we began.

It might be well to begin by summing up what we do know about the name *Bacchos* and its derivatives: We have a Semitic etymology for the name Bacchos but there is no known Semitic god or man so called. Conversely, we have the Lydian name *Baki-* etc. but no known Lydian etymology for that name. Similarly, we have the Greek name *Bacchos* etc. of god and men and the gentilician *Bacchiadai*. The Greek god's votaries, and occasionally, the god himself, are called *bacchoi* and *bacchai*, and their ritual activities are described by the verb *baccheuein*. The votaries sometimes bear *bacchic* or Bacchi(a)d names as their own personal names, although this practice seems not to have been especially common.[45] Both god and men exhibit the same range of onomastic variation: both are called *Bacchos, Baccheios, Baccheus* as well as *Bacchis*.[46] In addition to the Korinthian Bacchiad king, *Bacchis*, we hear of a *Bacchiad* at Delphi called *Bacchios* and also a *Bacchis*.[47] Although we cannot say for certain that every *Bacchic* name was in fact either Bacciad or bacchic (if these two categories are unconnected) or *genos* specific (if they are connected), it is quite probable, that they tended to be. This is a problem of a more general nature: in the Greek clans and families certain names tended to recur with a marked regularity; others obviously "surfaced" less often, but could remain latent in the clan down through the centuries. Clearly our data is far too limited to enable us to be precise. Enough, however, remains for us to make some plausible generalizations. In the nomenclature of the Neleid clan for example there is a remarkable recurrence of names which we can trace over at least a millennium from the Pylos tablets *via* Homer and Archaic Athens to the Ionian cities of Neleid foundation in the Hellenistic age. At Athens, a Megakles son of Megakles is almost certain to have been an Alkmeonid. What then are we to

---

[45] See e.g. the Agrippinilla inscription from Torre Nova, AJA, 37 (1933) 227 where the proper name Bacchis occurs twice, each time in a different ritual classification; cf. the name Bassaris id.

[46] The name Bucchis occurs several times in Alkaios; the context of fr. Z 11, LP seems to leave little doubt that the name is divine, cf. Et. Mag. s.v. Bucchis.

[47] Diod. 7.9.4. It is interesting in this connexion that we find Bakchiads in control of the oracle of Klarian Apollo, but we cannot speculate here about their possible connexion with the oracle at Delphi where Apollo's servants also had a role in the rites of the *roaring god*. Cf. also Soph. Ant. 1126f.

make of Bacchylides, the grandson of Bacchylides? The recurrence of a *Bacchic* name has led some to suspect a close connexion with Dionysiac cult (see RE s.v. Bakchylides). In our terms, however, this *run* indicates a recurrent pattern in the nomenclature of a particular *genos*, and happens also to contain the root *bakch-*, which is one of the denominators of that *genos*. The point is that it is the *genos* and not the individual and probably fortuitous carrier of the Bacchic name which has the special relationship with the god.

In addition, the name *Bacchis* was a common name for courtesans, and seems in fact to have been used as a kind of generic name denoting the professional capacities of its bearer rather like the name Lyde, for example, which could also be used to designate a bacchante[48]. Both god and man, then, slave and courtesan, commoner and king, could bear the Bacchic name. Everyone *adopted* into the ranks of the god Dionysos Bacchos was entitled to be called a *bacchos* or a *bacche*; few, however, actually bore the name of god and *genos* as their own personal name.

If we now consider the possible explanations of the *origin* of this most perplexing of names, we shall soon find that there are three of which two only are in fact at all plausible. We can dismiss the quite untenable notion straightaway: that the name *Bacchos* is in effect the result of pure onomastic inventiveness, a *nomen ex nihilo* or non-sense name; for we have already established the fact that the root *bacch-* is not Greek. The two remaining explanations are mutually exclusive: The first possibility is that the presence of the name *Bacchos* in Greece is the result of some complicated process of transmission – perhaps *via* Lydia in the final stage – from a foreign and probably ultimately Semitic source; the bacchic rites and the Bacchic name became an established part of Greek life, and the latter was even adopted by the Heraklid *genos* of Korinth who had formerly called themselves the Aletidai. To have done this the Korinthian Heraklids will have to have not only adopted a *kainon onoma*, but will have to have broken totally with the entrenched tradition of gentilician naming. In doing so they will have established a precedent which others might have followed; and yet we can point to no other clan who did. As we have already seen, however, there are *a priori* reasons for questioning this proposition. The alternative explanation which has received little or no scholarly consideration to date, is that both god and the Heraklid king of Korinth alike will have been called after *genos*. This means that the name *Bacchis* and all other formations from the root *Bacch-* will have been latent in the nomenclature of the Heraklid *genos* or of a particular branch of it. In other words the name will have existed in the *genos* not only before any particular historical individual *Bacchis vel sim*. But also before the god himself could be so named. The corollary of this supposition is

---

[48] See e.g. Ar., Thesm. 805, Eq. 765 ; cf. Athen. 594b; Plut. Mor. 753D.

that there will have been a particular *genos*, in this case called *Bacchi(a)d*, who were in charge of a particular set of rites, in this case *ta bakhika*. This phenomenon in itself is after all not unparalleled in ancient Greek society. What is perhaps different, even unique, here is the complexity of the rites, and the complex literary and artistic traditions attached to them as well of course as the various literary genres that evolved directly and indirectly from them.

We must consider first the obstacles, which are for the most part of a purely linguistic or onomastic nature, that are still in the way of the acceptance of this position. It would be well at this point to recall Burkert's enumeration of non-Greek names associated with the cult of Dionysos:

> *Mit Nichtgriechische ist zweifellos zu rechnen: Semele als Mutter, Bacchos als Name des Verehrers und Zweitname des Gottes, Thyrsos als sein heiliger Stab, Thriambos und Dithyrambos als sein Kultlied, dies sind offenbar lauter nicht griechische Wörter.*

He goes on to compare thyrsos with a god who is attested in Ugarit – *tirsu – Raschtrank* and with the late Hittite *tuwarsa Weinrebe*. These etimologies do indeed seem to have a certain Dionysiac appropriateness. But there are in fact a number of Greek names, related or identical, and Thracian ones, which could have been pointed to perhaps, from a Dionysiac standpoint, more profitably; for Thracians were closer to home in both time and space, and they were certain practitioners of Dionysiac orgiastic ritual. First thyrsos. The name exists in Greek;[49] it is commonly found in a particular genre of Greek poetry in the form *thyrsis*, and belongs certainly to a *Dorian* ambience if it is not in fact Heraklid.[50] But perhaps more interesting it occurs in compound formations in the names of Skyth and Thrako-Skyth kings who claimed Heraklid descent.[51] The name Semele occurs in an inscription from northern Greece; it is Thracian; this Semele is the perfectly mortal daughter of a Thracian named Torkos.[52] Perhaps most unexpected of all is the chance occurrence of the really rather bizarre name Dithyrhambos in the text of Herodotos; the name occurs also as a proper epithet of the god which, it is most plausible to assume, was historically prior to the common noun *dithyrhambos*. It is, however, the name of

---

[49] Iambl. V.P. 241 = DK 23 A 8; cf. Kaibel, Epigr. Gr. 127, 1.

[50] See e.g. Theokr. Id. I and Verg. Ec. VII.

[51] See Hdt. 4.76; cf. 4.10 and 4.79 for the connection with Skyles. The three Skyth and Thrako-Skyth children of Herakles are of interest in view of Herodotos' report of trieterides and baccheia among the remote Geloni. Skythes, the youngest of these sons is a name that recurs among prominent Dorians, e.g. Hdt. 7.163; here of course of especial interest is Skythes' son-Kadmos; cf. ib. 6.23. In addition to the personal name Idanthyrsos is the clan and personal name Agathyrsosoi.

[52] IG X 21. 926; the name may well have been traditional in her genos.

Harmatides, of the farther of Thespian Dithyrhambos which perhaps points once again in the Kadmeian direction. We might well suspect even at this early stage of *onomata* listing that the entire known world of classical antiquity was fairly infested with *Phoinicians*. What we must therefore suppose is that there were certain *shared names* which will have belonged to the two major racial-linguistic blocs of the Mediterranean world, namely the Semitic and the Indo-European. Some of these names have manifestly Semitic roots: Kadmos, Semele, Kabeiros, Labda, Labdakos, to name but a few; and of course, not least, Bacchos. Others certainly have suspiciously non-Indo-European sounding ones. It is strange considering the suspicion in which the Greek god Bacchos continues to be held, as regards his *Greekness*. Yet it was Phineus, Agenor's son, who held away over the shores of Thracian Salmydessos – a conjunction of three apparently Semitic names of which two are again specifically *Phoinician*. Numerous other examples could have been cited; but it will suffice here to note the pattern. There are several possible explanations for this rather considerable number of apparently Semitic names among both Greek and Thracian personal, tribal and place names. Either those names, which lack any obvious meaning in Greek but do yield a meaning if not a *meaningful* etymology from their apparently Semitic roots, are purely fortuitously Semitic-like words or these names belong to a very early linguistic *substratum*.

The habit of the Greek mind was to arrange onomastic *similia*, as indeed it did most *similia*, diachronically; this was a necessary ordering and a form of explanation. Seen in this light, the departure of Kadmos at the end of the *Bacchae* seems less puzzling: it obviously serves no ritual or dramatic purpose in terms of the play itself. But what it does do is to *mediate* between two sets of known *similia*, namely a set of identical names in both myth-historical and historical Thebes and in far away Illyria.[53] It is moreover a way of accounting for – in myth-historical terms – the historical change in the denominator of *genos* at Thebes: the Kadmeians or Agenoridai became the House of

---

[53] See Eur. Ba. 1330-39 and Dodds ad loc. It is perhaps worth adding that according to the present argument we would expect to find the practice of *bacchica* wherever Agenoridai were to be found. Indeed Dionysiac religion is otherwise attested for Illyria: the Epirote Olympias was an avid practitioner of the orgia and Dodona as we saw above was one of the places of the divine second birth of the god from the thigh of Zeus. Analogous to the travels and sojourns of Kadmos – but on a much grander scale – are those of Herakles; again this is a form of myth-historical explanation of known *similia* – branchs of Herakleidai or those claiming Heraklid descent, Greek and barbarian, in far-flung places.

Labdakos.[54] They did not cease to be in Thebes;[55] nor did they *begin* at Tyre. We must, it seems, simply accept the fact that certain names in a given language will mean nothing at all in that language and that they may mean something in a totally unrelated language. For our purposes it is not necessary to determine whether the large number of *Phointician* names in Greek is purely fortuitous or whether they point to a stage best described as Proto Indo-European Semitic, and are in effect frozen remnants due to extreme conservatism in tribal/gentilician nomenclatures. The name Charops, which is also a Greek word, occurs in Greece: in Homer it is *Trojan*, in Thrace it occurs in *Orphic* genealogy and in Illyria it is well attested as the name of Epirote kings and other important personages for centuries, sometimes in the spelling Tharops.[56] What is significant here is the fact that the name recurs in the nomenclatures of the *royal clans* of Illyria and Greece and in those of Troy and Thrace perhaps by analogy. These *royal* Charopoi will then have members of *basileia gene* in different countries, who may in fact have been kindred.

Now if etymologies are irrelevant in the case of some tribal names, we may well question whether they are not also in the case of others; for while the endless quest for "meaningful" etymologies of gods and men in antiquity more often than not results in success, that is in the unearthing of some plausible, or at least, possible, meaning for a given name, it is the efforts of scholars with the handful of names that will not yield anything at all credible that must alert us to the possibility that the entire approach is ill-founded and perhaps dangerously misleading. The principle adhered to in the present work is in fact the contrary one, namely that in the gentile nomenclatures of the Greeks in the names of their gods etymology is a matter of secondary importance; it was significant only after the fact; names were assigned *traditionally*, because they were a part of a system of names in a given *genos* – not because they carried a given meaning. It is further taken for granted that the majority of divine epithets are likewise *traditional*, that they somehow represent a given tribe, *genos* or family onomastically. This is by no means to deny that etymology was significant. Indeed it could hardly have been otherwise with the Greeks whose penchant for finding *etyma* was unquenchable. And in most cases they will not

---

[54] For the descent see Hdt. 5.59f.

[55] See e.g. Pind. Is.3.13f; EMagn. 215 shows the genos still intact and functioning in local *bacchica* .The Theban *trieterides* continued at least into the Hellenistic age and were celebrated in honour of Dionysos Kadmeios.

[56] It was in fact a name belonging to the "royal" clan of the Neleidai: the first decennial archon of Athens was named Charops; the names Charops and Charopos both occur on the Pylos tablets; cf. Hdt. 5.99 and Il.11.426; Diod. 3.65 (Here the Peisistratid-Neleid connections in the Pangaion region of Thrace may of significance); cf. Paus. 1.11; Thuch. 2.80.

have been disappointed; for most Greek names did mean something. But Dionysos Anthios or Euanthes for example was not so called because of any supposed connection with *flowers* or burgeoning spring, but because the name was traditional in the particular *genos* which assigned him the epithet.[57] Similarly he was Agrionios not because he and his votaries were *wild* but because both god and the Theban Trieterides celebrated in his honour which bore the specific feast name Argionia, will have been called after a branch of the Thrako-Paeonic tribe of Agrianes who were resident in Boeotia.

In cases where we find both god and *genos* called by the same name, or by a name that recurs with such frequency within the *genos* as to be an indicator of it, we must assume the onomastic priority of *genos*. Both gods and men, mountains, rivers and towns, bear the onomastic marks of *genos*. The sanctity of the name of genos is therefore a prior one. But we know that Dionysiac was called *Bacchos* virtually everywhere in the Greek world, by Dorians, by Ionians and by Aeolic-speaking peoples. If we cannot show a comparable distribution of a *Bacchic genos*, the assumption that the god's second name is gentiliacian in origin needs must founder.

Clearly within the confines of the present work it is not possible to present a comprehensive survey of Bacchiad diffusion in antiquity. But if we can show a well-defined distribution throughout the major tribal divisions of the Greeks, which would be something of an anomaly in itself, it will suffice. First, however, we might briefly consider the evidence for the connexion of bacchic ritual and *genos*. We know that in some places as late as Plutarch's day there were branchs of women (and men) who performed certain rituals at the trieteric festivals, who claimed descent from Bronze Age clans of Dionysiac myth-historical milleu. In the 1st century A.D. we hear of a priest of Dionysos at Thera, where the location of the cult strongly suggests the trieteric-orgiastic form of worship.

We know that the ruling clan of post-*Kadmeian* Thebes were the Labdakidai who traced their descent back to Agenor's son, Kadmos.[58] At some point political hegemony will have passed to some other Theban clan, and the Labdakidai will have lost their power and their splendour. But from Hellenistic inscriptions we know that Trieterides continued to be celebrated at Thebes in

---

[57] Particularly instructive is Hes. Fr. 283 M.W.; cf. school. ad Ap. Rh. 3.997. Cf. also Paus. 1.31.4; Athen. 465B; Paus. 7.21.6 where Antheus – *flowery* is one of three *onomata* belonging to both three images of the god and three ancient towns at Patrai. The second two mean nothing: Euanthes was also a Lokrian noble who led a colony (Strab. 6.270). This is of interest because the Lokrians were early colonisers of Abdera on the south Thracian coast in the territory of the Thracian tribe of Bistonians who were related to the Kikonians of Ismaros (Chian Maroneia): they continued into Roman times to send maenads to Ismaros to celebrate joint orgia *eis oros*.

[58] See Paus. 2.6.2f.

honour of Dionysos Kadmeios, and from the Magnesia inscription we deduce that there was still in the Hellenistic age a clan at Thebes who were active in Dionysiac *service* and who traced their descent from *Kadmeian* (or Agenorid) Ino. This clan will have been the Labdakidai – or some now nameless branch of it.[59] We shall see below how the name Labdakos connects the ruling House of Thebes with the Bacchiadai of Korinth.

Perhaps we are now in position to posit a plausible *terminus ante quem* for this practice of *bacchic colonisation* from the Theban metropolis. Tradition tells of a marriage alliance between the royal houses of *sandy Pylos* and Kadmeian Thebes. *Naleus* took Chloris for his wife, the daughter of Amphion king of Thebes. His surname was Labdakides. One thing is clear: if Thebes sent out women of the House of Labdakos to Pylos or to other places in Bronze Age Greece, these will have been in effect *carriers* of the bacchic form of Dionysiac religion – whatever the purpose of the transactions. But in case of the Pylian Neleids we find that Labdakid (Agenorid) names continue to penetrate the clan's nomenclature as late as the 5th century B.C. when the Milesian Neleid, Peisistratos, the son of Agenor, was Aisymnetes.[60] It is therefore unlikely on the basis of this limited amount of onomastic evidence and on *a priori* grounds as well that there will have been only one Labdakid involved with the Neleids of Pylos. In fact the tradition which tells of the marriage alliance itself may simply reflect some form of Agenorid – Neleid bonding – or pattern of *dual organisation* translated into "historical terms": to explain in terms of *Herkunft* the *origins* of a kinship system within which one clan, *basileion genos*, is paired with another clan who are in the category of *strangers*.[61] But the important point to be underlined here is that the demand for Agenorid blood or lineages from what was certainly the major store-house (but not the only one) of bacchic blood in Greece presupposes an established norm which had to be maintained: If in one place a lineage ceased altogether, it had to be replaced; if in another

---

[59] See Pind. Is. 3.13ff.

[60] In this connexion the very tradition recorded by Herodotos (1.70) concerning the hypothetical Phoinician "origin" of the Mileasian Thales is of some interest. Of particular importance for the theory of "dual organization" is the phrase… *epolithgrafethē de (Agēnōr) en Milētō hote ēlthe syn Neileōi ekpesonti Foinikēs* id. There was an early historian who wrote about the foundation of Miletos, named Kadmos. Here we can only note in passing a possible connection of some importance: the ruling family of Akragas were descended from the Emmenidai who were descended from *Kadmos*, Pind. Ol. 2.16-47. These in turn were allied with the rulers of Bacchiad Syrakuse.

[61] The very names of Neleus' mother, Tyro, and her father, Salmoneus, suggest *Phoinician Herkunft*; but when translated into terms of kinship categories, they would seem to point to a form of "dual organization" existing prior to the clan *Stammvater* Neleus.

place the lineages were in danger of depletion, they had to be replenished and so on.

The major obstacle in the way of determining Bacchiad diffusion in antiquity both synchronically and diachronically is the fact that changes did take place in the denominators of *gene* quite generally. Hesiod, for example, can speak of the Amythaonidai who are distinguished by their *nous*. But the clan are normally throughout antiquity, regardless of place, reffered to as the Melampodidai. Other clans were subject, however, to rather some numerous changes in clan name – either for internal or for external causes. The branch of *Heraklidai* who went to Korinth and became known subsequently as the Aletidai are one; these, then, five generations later became known as the *Bacchiadai*. After the expulsion of the clan from Korinth one branch went north and became known as the Lynkestians.

We find that Labdakid (Agenorid) names continue to penetrate the clan's nomenclature as late as the 5th century B.C. when the Milesian Neleid, Peisistratos, the son of Agenor, was Aisymnetes. It is therefore unlikely on the basis of this limited amount of onomastic evidence and on a priori grounds as well that there will have been only one Labdakid involved with the Neleids of Pylos. In fact the tradition which tells of the marriage alliance itself may simply reflect some form of Agenorid – Neleid bonding –or pattern of *dual organisation* translated into *historical terms*: to explain in terms of *Herkunft* the *origins* of a kinship system within which one clan, *basileion genos*, is paired with another clan who are in the category of *strangers*.[62] But the important point to be underlined here is that the demand for Agenorid blood or lineages from what was certainly the major store-house (but not the only one) of bacchic blood in Greece presupposes an established norm which had to be maintained: If in one place a lineage ceased altogether, it had to be replaced; if in another place the lineages were in danger of depletion, they had to be replenished and so on. By this reasoning the *terminus ante quem* for the existence of the norm itself will simply be *uralt*. Another group, according to tradition, went to Etruria where they established the Tarquin dynasty in the next generation. Thus both internal events as well as emigration can bring about a change in clan name.

At Thebes we may plausibly deduce at least three changes in the denominator of the bacchic clan: Agenoridai, Kadmeioi (which is not a proper one) and Labdakidai. Ino for example was called *Kadmeis* in the Magnesia inscription elsewhere she is Agenoris.[63] In a fragmentary tomb inscription from the

---

[62] The very names of Neleus' mother, Tyro, and her father, Salmoneus, suggest *Phoinician origin*; but when translated into terms of kinship categories, they would seem to point to a form of "dual organization" existing prior to the clan *Stammvater* Neleus.

[63] Opp., Kyn. 4.237; Hyg., Fab. 4.2 and Nonnos, D., 9.285ff.

island of Tenos a "maenad of wild Bromios" participates in the rites of the Agēnorid[.[64] Leda's father, Thestios, was the son of Agenor; and indeed the Thestiadai were a Tenian tribe.[65] There was also a shrine of Agenor's son Kadmos and two of his descendants in the heart of Sparta. Finally, Dionysos was himself called Agenoreus in some places.[66] It is, however, at Thebes alone that the name Labdakos which will have been latent in the nomenclature of the Agenorid clan, became the clan denominator. [67]This name does come to the surface as far as we know only once again in the nomenclature of one other clan, the Bacchiadai of Korinth[68]. That it was, however, nor insignificant in Bacchiad nomenclature may be inferred from the fact that the same root occurs in a place name in Bacchiad Syrakuse.

Individual names in the systems of names of different clans can tell us a great deal if, like Labda and Labdakos, they are sufficiently uncommon. But a run of two generations of names can obviously tell us more that is certain, and in fact often sufficient to indicate *genos*. If the names Labda and Labdakos do not suffice on their own to connect the clans of Korinth and Thebes, certainly the combination of Labda Amphionis and Amphion Labdakides is persuasive.[69] For Amphion, while by no means as unusual as Labda, is not at all common in the *corpus* of Greek names. Again in the two same clans the name Aktaion occurs, significantly, in both cases in contexts of myth-ritual or mock ritual *sparagmos*.[70] The father of Korinthian Aktaion, Melissos, again shares his name with the men from the Theban clan of Labdakidai; but Theban Aktaion's father was Aristaios – a name that is most intriguing because of its Dionysiac associations in Dorian, Aeolic and Ionian places as we shall see below. But it is not only the coincidence of *onomata* that links the ruling houses of Korinth and Thebes; it is also myth: the Oidipous saga in particular.[71] Oidipous, the grandson of Labdakos, belongs in some fashion to both Korinthian and Theban royal houses. The story is of course among other things about *incest*; but it is also about endogamy.[72]

[64] IG 12.5.972 (2nd C A.D.) = Kaibel, Epigr. Gr. 871.

[65] CIG 2338, 78.83:

[66] See e.g. Stat. Achil. I 693ff. Lucus Agenorei sublimis ad orgia Bacchi/stabat,…

[67] There are of course mythological adumbrations of *sparagmos* in connexion with Labdakos who is said to have perished "because he was like-minded with Pentheus', (Apollod.) 3.5.4f.

[68] See Hdt. 5.92.

[69] See Hdt. 5.92; for the family tree at Thebes see Paus. 2.6.1ff. and Hdt. 5.59.

[70] See e.g. Eur. Ba. 1127 and 1291 and see Dodds 1960 ad ib. 337-40.

[71] But see also Paus. 2.6 where *Polybos* is a Sikyonian and there are other Theban protagonists.

[72] See e.g. Eur. Phoin. 21f. In effect the Labdakidai will have been endogamous so long as they were a *royal clan*: cf. the Bacchiadai of Korinth.

Before we turn away from the question of Theban-Korinthian connections entirely, it would be well to note in passing one further tie that is especially intriguing. We know from an early and reliable source that at some time during the Archaic age a Korinthian Bacchiad named Philolaos went to Thebes to act as law-maker for the Thebans.[73] This fact alone of course need not imply anything at all about family connexions. It becomes interesting, however, when we recall the activities of Pythagoras himself in Southern Italy, and when he remember that Philolaos, one of the most important of the early Pythagoreans, spent some time, according to Plato, teaching at Thebes.[74] Unfortunately, for our purposes the epithet Pythagoreios (which is comparable in form to Kadmeios, an epithet which often obscures the proper Agenorid or Labdakid gentilician name) has obscured his real gentilician. Here, however, the Bacchiad Philolaos can perhaps assist us; for Philolaos can perhaps assist us; for Philolaos again is a relatively rare name which will have belonged to a system of Bacchiad names: it will have recurred in previous generations and would recur regularly in succeeding generations of Bacchiadai, although we can only guess at the degree of regularity. In spite of the fact then that we do not know whether the name was absolutely genos specific, we may plausibly conjecture that Philolaos Pythagoreios will have been either a Bacchiad or a member of a clan who were bonded with Bacchiads which would account for the penetration of a Bacchiad name in the nomenclature of a non-Bacchiad clan. If the equation proposed above, namely, that the Theban Labdakidai and Korinthian Bacchiadai were different branches of the same clan with different names, is correct, then we can more easily understand the activities of Philolaos Bacchiades at Thebes (and perhaps, by analogy, those of Pythagoras at Kroton).

Korinthian Bacchiad–Theban relations would cease by definition after the Bacchiad diaspora. But beginning at the latest in the late 5th century B.C. we find a nexus of *intellectual relations* between the Pythagorean cities of Southern Italy, notably Metapontum and Kroton, and Thebes and Phlios from which Pythagoras' ancestors had emigrated to Samos.[75] And it is just in the realm of Dionysiac religion that we can connect Thebes with early Korinth and

---

[73] Aristot. Pol. 1274; there are adumbrations of endogamy (*incest*) at Korinth in the very explanation Aristotle transmits.

[74] Phd. 61E; he will have been resident in Thebes sometime before 399 B.C.

[75] We learn that the Pythagorean Philolaos had relatives at Syrakuse (D.L. 8.84 = DK 44 A1.), and we may plausibly deduce that these will have been Bacchiadai. On the emigration of Pythagoras' ancestors from Phlios see Paus. 2.13.2; As Burkert says (1972, 206, n. 77) it is hardly an accident that the uncommon name Hippasos appears in both; but it is Bacchiad-Agenorid nomenclature that is responsible. Interestingly, it was the child Hippasos, son of Leukippe, who was the victim of *sparagmos* at Boeotian Orchomenos. The Leukippidai were a clan or family of maenads at Sparta, Paus. 3.13.7

Phlios via Sikyon,[76] where local tradition linked the Sikyonian Dionysos, named *Baccheios* with Phlian Androdamas. And with the exception of Naxos, it is in these three places alone in all of Greece that a tangible image of the god bore the name *Baccheios*. In spite of the fact that Dionysos was worshipped as *Baccheios* or *Bacchos* etc., throughout the Greek world and in spite of the fact that these small cult statues, whatever the substance of their composition, abounded – and very often in pairs – in the towns and villages of the Greeks, it is only at Korinth, at Sikyon and, by deduction, at Phlias, (and Naxos) that we find them called Baccheios. It cannot be coincidence that this was Bacchiad territory and that these were important centres for the early history of the dithyrhamb. It remains only to point out that Androdamas is associated with a period well before the probable of Bacchis, son of Proumnis; and most important, we deduce from this that at this level of cult, the epithet was not transferable to non-Bacchiad *gene*. The entire complex can be explained by the fact of Bacchiad endogamy: whereas the norm in most places in Greece will have been a *royal clan* or later its fictive counterpart, and a Bacchic clan with whom they will have been paired and with whom they will have jointly controlled Dionysiac ritual, which comprised the *bacchica*, on the other hand, at Korinth and seemingly, at one time at Sikyon and Phlios, there will have been a *royal clan* and the paired clan both with Bacchic proper names.

This information, then, combined with our knowledge of the Theban sojourn of both these *sophoi* called Philolaos, may well point to family connections at Thebes, and seems to support the inference that Philolaos Pythagoreios was in fact a *Bacchiad* – or a member of a clan with whom the Bacchiadai were bonded. And this in turn would help us make sense of an apparent anomaly: the appearance among the list of the Pythagorean Philolaos' writings of the title Bacchai.[77] Indeed we might well expect the heavily Dorian area of Greater Greece which played host to Pythagoras during the last half of his life, to be a stronghold of Dionysiac religion. Sophokles in fact represents Sicily and South Italy as a kind of second head-quarters of the Dionysiac *church* in the century or so after Pythagoras.[78]

Herodotos merely confirms the view of his friend, the poet, when he represents " the Pythagoreans, as the *brains* behind bacchic ritual and *theology*. Bacchic they may well have been in name and associated almost universally with the Thracian Orpheus to whom was ascribed the bulk of theogonic and theological literature – most, but not all of it, Dionysiac. Not all our evidence attesting Bacchiad diffusion is quite so inaccessible: There were *Bacchiadai*

---

[76] See Paus. 2.7.6.

[77] Fr. 17 = Stob. 1.15.7; see Burkert, 1972, 269, n. 148

[78] (Ant. 1117 f.)

living at Delphi under that name as we have seen above. At Athens we can even connect them with Dionysiac religion.[79] These are an isolated pair. But it is very tempting indeed to see in the so-called *Iobaccheia* which were *traditional* (*kata ta patria*) in the 4th century B.C., rites that ere gentilitial in origin, i.e., originally the preserve of a particular genos or family at Athens.[80] And in turn we might plausibly connect with these, the long intervening silence of the stones notwithstanding, the bacchic society of men in Athens in the Imperial age who called themselves the *Iobacchoi*. Here it is instructive to recall that Dionysos was *Iobacchos* specifically at Delphi; and it was to Delphi that Athenian women went every second year to celebrate the *Trieterides* with the local women called Thyiads.[81] It would not be germane to our purpose here to speculate about the precise nature of the rites called *Iobaccheia* nor about any possible connexion (or identity) between the group of priestesses who administered them, the so-called Gerairai, and the group of Athenian Thyiads who participated in the Delphic *Trieterides*, however interesting and important the question is. What is, however, of special interest for us is the onomastic doublet in the *Oath of the Gerairai*.[82] Dionysos Theoinos is associated specifically with maenadism; and we know that there was also at Athens a *genos* which bore that name. If both names are in fact of gentilician origin as seems highly probable, then we should have also for Athens strong indications of the kind of clan pairing or bonding we have been considering throughout as a probable model. In this context the group of Bacchiadai who are said to have gone north to Lynkestis at the time of the diaspora are particularly relevant: For the daughters of the princes of Lynkestis married into the Macedonian royal line. Once again then the pattern of a *royal clan* bonded with a Bacchic clan – in this case known *Bacchiadai* – is clear. A chance notice among the endless lists of culinary delights described by Athenaios preserves for us yet another *royal*-bacchic doublet – this time couched explicitly in terms of traditional Macedonian sacrificial symposia.[83]

The last major centre of Bacchiad concentration we will consider here is Miletos. Hesychios is our most explicit witness: according to him Bacchiadai

---

[79] CIA, iii, 97.

[80] See (Dem.) in Neaeram 73-78.

[81] Paus. 10.4.3; cf. ib. 10.6.4 and 10.32.6f.

[82] Hagisteuō kai eimi kathara kai hagnē... kai ta Theoinia kai ta Iobakheia gerarō tōi Dionysōi kata ta patria kai tois kathekousi hronois. Above for the oath of the Gerairai . On Dion.Theoinos see schol. ad Lykophr. 1247.

[83] Athen. xiv 659f. In several of her publications Tacheva comes to the conclusion that that the cult of Zeus Hypsistos in Ancient Macedonia is mostly a royal cult associated with the Argeads and, possibly, with the representatives of the generic aristocracy (see Taceva-Hitova, 1983, 177ff).

were to be found not only at Korinth but also at Miletos. The notice is short and unambiguous. Bacchiadai were then to be found in relatively large numbers of Miletos; they were genetically and onomastically intact; furthermore, since the Milesian branch of the clan were selected for special mention, we may plausibly infer that they will have played some specially significant or additional role in this *prima facie* alien community. And indeed we learn from other sources that they did in fact hold an important position within the nexus of Ionian – or Neleid – geo-political and *religious* relations: They were in control of the Klarian oracle of Apollo.[84] From this fact we easily infer that their residence at Miletos in the heart of alien tribal territory and their control of this oracle which was important to both Miletos and Ephesos either will have antedated Neleid settlement of this area or they will have settled it jointly with the Neleidai. It is virtually certain that their arrival will not have been subsequent to that of Neleids.

The orgiastic form of Dionysiac religion is particularly well attested for this areas; and it has been conjectured that Dionysos was somehow connected also with the oracle itself. This does not come as a surprise; for he is connected in numerous ways with the oracle of Apollo at Delphi; there was even a tradition which placed the *roaring god* there first.[85] Besides Dionysos had his own oracle in Greece – and several at least in Thrace.[86] And it is in Thrace that we find the nearest analogue to the situation at Klaros: the Thracian tribe of Satrai were in possession of an oracle of Dionysos *on the highest mountains*, but the *Bessoi of the Satrai* were in charge of the oracle.[87] The expression is puzzling, though not unintelligible: If Herodotos had meant that the Bessoi were a clan belonging to the tribe of Satrai, he would not have eschewed the word *genos*. The Bessoi here are linked with Satrai: they live and serve as priests among them but are not of their lineage.[88]

Both the form of *genos* pairing or *dual organisation* described above and the widespread diffusion of one of the paired gene have their analogues of partial parallels in other ancient cultures and in modern primitive ones. It is interesting that the classical scholar Perdrizet long ago drew a similar comparison with the ubiquitous Thracian Bessoi which he called *les levites du Bacchos*

---

[84] See Nikand. Alex. 11 and schol.ad. loc. Manto is connected with Delphi as well as Kolophon, schol. ad Ap. Rh. 1.308. At Korinth too Apollo was Klarios. Of particular interest is Tac. Ann. 2.54.

[85] Schol. Ad Pind. Pyth. hypoth., 297.

[86] At Amphikleia in Phokis the nexus of orgiastic and oracular ritual was Dionysiac (Paus. 10.33.10) as in Thrace; see e.g. Hdt. 7.111; Eur. Hek. 1267; Rh. 967-73.

[87] Hdt. 7.111.

[88] See Fol, 1991, 161; Delev 2014, 167ff.

Thrace.[89] Perdrizet thus elaborated a theory of gentilician diffusion for Thrace. He followed Creuzer in derivating the ethnonym Bessi from the root *Bassaros, Bassarai.* The latter were thought to derive from a hypothetical Thracian word meaning *fox,* and to point to a time when – in accordance with *la zoolatrie totemoue* – the tribe were tattooed with the sign of the fox. There is little purpose here in delivering the customary structures about theories of *totemism*: for in any case according to the position adopted throughout the present work the meaning of the word *Bassaros* is not very relevant. But the purported relation between the names *Bessoi* and *Bassaros* etc., is a matter of the utmost interest. For *Bassarai* was the generic name for the Thracian female votaries of the god, as *Bacchai* was for the Greek ones; indeed the Bessoi do seem to have been a special class of Dionysiac devotees and priests. And like the Bacchiadai of Klaros they were in charge of oracles in Thrace – one certainly and probably more.

We have seen sufficient evidence by now to have some general idea of the extent of Bacchiad diffusion in the Greek world: it was considerable. And we have seen that the pattern itself has its parallels in other cultures, ancient and modern primitive. The Thracian parallel is of course the closest in time and geographical proximity; it is little short of striking, however, because it involves the same god. The nature of the Greek evidence is such as to fairly invite us to speculate about an *Urdiffusion,* and about a series of subsequent periods of contraction and concentration, as for example at Korinth, followed by periods of further diffusion and redistribution. Certainly it has been shown that Bacchiad diffusion in the historical period we have been considering was sufficient to satisfy the preconditions of the theory proposed above: that the *bacchica* were attached to a particular *genos* and that that *genos* was, *ceteris paribus,* called Bacchic.

One of the major and least questioned assumptions of the communis opinio which touches upon both the issue of the god's nature and of his origins, is that Dionysos is a god of the lower orders. This inference is predicated upon the following points or premises: (1) Homer's apparent relative silence shows a lack of intimate awareness or a lack of interest and disdain.(2) Initiation into the Dionysiac mysteries was apparently open to slaves and in general to the lower and *fringe* members of Greek society, whereas the attraction of the rich and well-born was seemingly late. (3)The increase in Dionysiac activity and information coincides roughly with the rise of the *democratic* tyrannies (here the name of Peisistratos is always to the fore), and the fostering of the Dionysiac arts is somehow construed for the Greek *dēmos.* (4) Dionyos is the god of fertility, orgiastic and mystic rites which it seems are thought of as of particular

---

[89] See Perdrrizet, 1910, 39.

relevance to these orders, if not in fact their exclusive preoccupation. Jaeger expresses very similar views:

> *But in the course of the social upheaval caused by the wide-spread class struggles… which were to reach their peak during the sixth century, the social and political rise of the lower classes was accompanied also by the penetration of their religious conceptions into the higher intellectual life, thus smoothing the way for decisive changes. This revolution was heralded by the mounting esteem in which the cult of Dionysos now came to be held. Even as late as the Homeric (…..) this cult had hardly been deemed worth considering; now, however, it began to spread from the plains to the cities (2), where it soon found a place in the public festivals and divine ceremonies. Originally the orgiastic character of the Dionysiac religion had been looked upon as something quite alien, an insult all municipal order…*[90]

For Jaeger then this putative *recognition* of the god seems to be not only an effect of the revolution of the sixth century, but almost a contributory cause. Indeed it is not surprising that it is this aspect of Dionysiac religion which is prominently referred to and discusses in the works of social anthropologists and social historians leading in the most cases to wildly misleading or erroneous comparisons: recently the cult of Dionysos has been compared – in the *appeal it held for women and for men of low social status*. Among recent accounts in histories of Greek religion one finds little or no modification of this basic view:

> *to Homer and his society Dionysos was of no importance. He had nothing to say to a race of aristocrats.*[91]

A.B. Dietrich carries it several steps further in terms of historiography:

> *The cult of Dionysos in fact in 6th C Athens became respectable, and was observed by all classes in society. The god of the lower orders, as it were, concerned with fertility, orgiastic and mystic rites, had been known to the Homeric poets but was neglected by them. Much of his myth reflected the vigour with which the nobility resisted the introduction of Dionysiac cult. However, it was the achievement of Peisistratos and his successors that reconciliation came about between the religious cult of the lower classes and the city gods, the gods of the aristocracy. Dionysos ascent to the ranks of the Olympians during this period can be judged by the god's becoming the*

---

[90] See Jaeger, 1936, 57f.
[91] See Guthrie, 1950,160.

favourite subject of the Attic vase painters, and by the temple which was built to Dionysos in Athens in the last years of the sixth century.

There are at least three difficulties here: first the conclusion that Dionysos achieved a new and improved status during the rule of the Peisistratids is based upon highly questionable foundations; for while focusing on the cult of Dionysos Eleuthereus, which was indisputably a late import for which there are numerous alternative explanations to the one taken for granted here, Dietrich has neglected Dionysos Lenaios, whose cult is universally acknowledged to have been an old one, and was the cult of the *kings* of Athens. But an addition is seen as a *rise*; and the putative *rise* itself is based upon a logical fallacy – *post hoc ergo propter hoc*: since trends were generally in the direction of *democratisation*, anything seen to be given sudden prominence is deemed *democratic*. In fact it is just during the 6th century that our sources on most aspects of Greek life and society begin to increase dramatically. While there can be little doubt that Dionysos and his retinue were among the favourite subjects of the 6th century Attic vase-painters, as evidence for the putative *volte face* which turned the god of the *lower orders* into a *respectable Olympian*, who would no longer offend aristocratic sensibilities, it is useless. In addition to these more or less formal arguments against the democratic' interpretation of Dionysiac religion and its rapid and dramatic growth under the fostering tyrants of the Archaic period, we might examine the same proposition in the longer, historical, light of gentilician continuities. We will recall that the Athenian Peisistratos was one of the principal props in the *democratic* view: the favouring of the *people's* god and of Dionysiac arts is seen as the clever stratagem of an ambitious aristocrat; the *adoption* of Dionysiac religion as the official *state-religion* as a means of readjusting political alliances for the purpose of personal aggrandisement. It is not at all odd given the past and the current preconceptions about the nature of Dionysiac religion and its history that the question of Peisistratid tribal and gentilician affiliations has never been posed in this context. Yet *genos* is a matter of quite general import in the study of Greek cults and in this particular case one of vital interest. For the Peisistratidai boasted of their Neleid decent. And the Neleidai were unquestionably aristocratic. They were in fact a remarkable clan: very old and continuous. We can in fact establish a kind of Dionysiac chronology by focusing upon this one clan in their many and far-flung homes. For almost everywhere we find Neleids, we find the god Dionysos – in the Bronze Age remains of *sandy Pylos*, on the banks of the now dry Ilissos, in the great cities of Ionian Asia Minor which claimed Neleid foundation – Miletos, Priene, Ephesos – and in Mileasian Olbia on the northern shores of the Euxine. In at least one place, Miletos, we can establish almost certain ritual continuity throughout the centuries of Neleid hegemony; and in Milesian prosopography we can perhaps discern Neleid involvement in Dionysiac cult *at the top* long after the clan had ceased to govern more or less exclusively, and after access to the major Dionysiac priesthoods had been opened up.[92] Perhaps a word is in order here about the discrepancies in the class of the various categories of Dionysiac votaries, in particular, between *Bacchai* and *Bacchoi*. The former are *semnai* – the wives and the daughters of *kings*; the former change their status upon marriage into the *royal* from the non-royal, bacchic clan in our hypothetical model. The men of the bonded, bacchic, clan, however, never change their status; and short of resorting to endogamous systems, were never *royal*. They were therefore according to the constraints imposed by the Hellenic system of kinship organisation, traditionally and categorically non-aristocratic. Thus while both female and male baccheia will have been in some sense *democratic* in its programme of initiations, the official *bacchai* of any given place will have been *aristocratic* while the official *bacchoi* will have been non-aristocratic; Changing political circumstances and the breakdown of a rigid kinship system would leave *branchs* of *bacchoi* – non-aligned and therefore even *stranger*, denigrated by some and despised by others, but tolerated, it would seem, almost everywhere.

It is moreover certain, as we shall see below, that the Milesians (and almost certainly other Neleid cities) celebrated the *trieterides* duringwhich they held their *baccheia*, and that these *trieterides* and *baccheia* were attached to the cult of the Leniad Dionysos. It has long been generally acknowledged that the Lenaian festival at Athens must have attended the *Ionian settlement*. There is little point then in endeavouring to trace by a series of painstaking deductions this same festival back to its probable origins. It will suffice to say that if it belonged to sub-Mycenaen Athens, and if it was presided over by the dynasty of Medontid kings who traced their descent from Pylian Neleids, itwould be inexplicable if the festival had not been celebrated at Pylos. But it is not the antiquity of the festival, but rather the prominence and the importance of the role the Archon Basileus in it which needs underlining here: the *king* was in charge of the *pompe* and the *agon*, and, most significantly, it was he who made all the

---

[92] An Hellenistic tomb epigram names the leader of the official Bacchai of the city as Alkmeonis. The name Alkmeon almost certainly belongs to the Neleid nomenclature of the Milesian branch of the clan: the Aisymnetes in 457/6 was Alkmeon, son of Hipparchos. We cannot consider here the obviously relevant issue of the purported Neleid descent of the Athenian family of the Alcmeonidai and their close ties with Delphi and Apollo's temple where the bones of Dion. were laid, and where the Hosioi performed an *unmentionable sacrifice* when the Thyiads awakened Liknites. See Henrichs, 1978, 121-160

arrangements for the traditional sacrifices.[93] Certainly for no other god are there such clear and present *semeia*, or so many, of concrete ritual links between god and the royal houses of Hellas: Dionysos not only "moved in the best society", he was served by kings. In addition, the ritual marriage and intercourse of the Basilinna with the god will have regularly and repeatedly re-established the claim of that *genos*, collectively, and of her own offspring, individually, to divine descent – descent from the god Dionysos.[94]

We might easily call the Lenaia a Neleid festival; for it was Neleids who, according to tradition, founded most of the major cities of Ionian Asia Minor.[95] There the festival survived well into the Empire; there, there is ample testimony not only to its longevity, but to its continued vigour. There, too, there are clearer signs both of its complex nature and of the extent of its contours. The Athenian Medontidai were for centuries the principal ritual participants in the Lenaian festival; and it is these descendants of Pylian kings who handed on their god to their more democratic successors. But it was the fictive counterparts of these kings (at Athens at least), the Kings-archons, who continued to control the winter offices of the *roaring god*. Nothing is better evidence of the former glory of the god or of the centre position of orgiastic Dionysiac religion in the early state.

---

[93] See Aristot. Ath. Pol. LVII. I. Cf. Poll. VIII, 90; IG 2. 2130. 57ff.
[94] See Aristot. ib. III. 5.
[95] According to tradition Neleus founded Miletos, Hdt. 9.97;

CHAPTER II

OREIBASIA. SOME NOTES
ON THE THRACIAN ORGIA

A favorite assumption of the *communis opinio* holds that at some time there had been a *channeling* of this wild, *irrational* and above all, foreign, cult which took place on Greek soil; with reputation came a diminution of Dionysiac *savagery* which is perhaps most conspicuous in the *raw feasts* of the god's votaries. Here too, however, the evidence for the supposed, *primal state* of Dionysiac savagery is the myths, although most scholars do not countenance the idea of a time when human, rather than animal, flesh was the ritual staple. Thus Dionysiac myth and certain supposed attenuations of barbaric practices like omophagy or *primitive* states like the ecstasies of *hoi bakcheuontes*, which do not accord with our presuppositions about the nature of *to Hellenikon*, have encouraged scholars to speak about the evolution of modification of ritual practice with reference to *a starting point* or hypothetical "early stage" which is deduced from myth. The reasoning is of course entirely circular.

Here, our concern will be the matter of Thracian (or Thrako-Phrygian) *origins* only as it relates specifically to the question of periodicity. Farnell[96] had long ago been aware that the Thracian rites were indeed characterized by the same periodicity as the Greek ones. He had in fact quite ingeniously devised an explanation that would account for the biennial rhythm and at the same time underline the Thracian origin of the Greek rites: the biennial periodicity was due to the hypothetical Thracian practice of *crop rotation*. At the same time the obvious discrepancy of a *dying* or *fertility god* who returned only every second year to the upper world was apparently thought to have been got rid of; such a creature would "naturally" be attached to the agricultural cycle – an annual one – which the advanced science of the backward Thracian altered.[97] The implications of this evidence are of the utmost significance: there can be no thought of control or *canalization*, whether by Delphi or any other Greek institution, of Thracian Dionysiac ritual. Clearly we must regard the biennial rhythm as proper to the rites themselves and not as a pattern imposed from the outside – certainly not as one more example of the Greek culture for imposing order and rationality upon the chaotic and irrational.

---

[96] See Farnel L., 2004.

[97] For Dionysos as a Thracian god see also: Rapp 1882; Perdrzet 1910; Wilamowitz II, 61f; Nilsson 1950, 568f; Picard, 1946, 455-473; Preller-Robert, 1894, 659ff; Guthrie, 1950, ch. 6.; Михаилов, 1972, Венедиков 1983, 129ff; Маразов, 2000; Фол, 1991, 2002

The tendency, introduced by the student of Dionysiac religion, Rohde[98], to explain and elucidate its peculiar and apparently unhellenic characteristics by appealing to *prima facie* similar phenomena in totally unrelated societies has produced some unfortunate results. But most important, it had deflected our attention away from perhaps more productive lines of enquiry and even clouded our apprehension of certain obvious and significant facts. Following in this tradition Dodds[99] adduced a number of parallels – most of them historical – in his highly influential introduction to *Bachae* of Euripides. Speaking of the outbreaks of *dancing madness* which afflicted Europe periodically beginning in the fourteenth century and which it seems in some places *crystalized into annual festivals* he continues:

> *This last fact suggests the way in which in Greece the ritual at a fixed date may originally have developed out of spontaneous attacks of mass hysteria. By canalizing such hysteria in an organized rite once in two years, the Dionysiac cult kept it within bounds and gave it a relatively harmless outlet. What the parodos of the Bacchae depicts is hysteria subdued to the service of religion.*

In the matter of *canalizing* then Dodds is at one with Nock[100] who in the following account explicitly links this issue of periodicity with that of the *origins* of the cult:

> *Dionysos is above all gaining in this period (sc. The Archaic), and the story of his cult affords the most manifest example of religious conquest. It represents a religious invasion from the Thraco-Phrygian stock. The adherents of Dionysos, mainly women, wandered on mountain sides. They were called by various names such as Maenads and Bacchae indicating their spiritual union with the god... The coming of this into Greek life seems to have produced one of those outbreaks of religious frenzy which at times spread like fever (such for instance was the Flagellant movement)... This movement was canalized by Delphi, itself now the bulwark of religious conservatism: Dionysos was given three months of the year at Delphi itself, an different cities had their regular Maenads... What had been a liberation for all became a formal annual performance by a few women, taking its place in the ordinary cycle of regular rites.*

---

[98] See Rhode, 1987.
[99] See Dodds, 1960, XIV *There must have been a time when the maenads or thyiads really became for a few hours or days what their name implies – wild women whose human personality has been temporarily replaced by another.*
[100] See Nock, 1972, 54.

Thus once again we have in essence the tale told by the myths: foreign encroachment, resistance and conquest by an alien, divine Dionysiac force. What the myths do omit, however, the historian supplies, namely the theory of the *conversation* of the invading cult by the *invaded*.

The implications of this evidence are of the utmost significance: there can be no thought of control or *channeling*, whether by Delphi or any other Greek institution, of Thracian Dionysiac ritual. Clearly we must regard the biennial rhythm as proper to the rites themselves and not as a pattern imposed from the outside – certainly not as one more example of the Greek genius for imposing order and rationality upon the chaotic and irrational. Of the notion of "hysteria" (in the sense that it is used by Dodds and Nock) as something native to maenadism – proper and essential to it in its *earlier stages* – we must ask whether it does not in fact betray a deep misunderstanding of the very nature of ritual. For "ritual hysteria" has nothing to do with spontaneous eruptions which, however susceptible to explanation by the social or political historian, come out of the blue, in disorder and are uncontrolled. *Ritual hysteria* on the other hand is controlled, formulate, even, alas, orderly. Above all we must categorically reject the notion of *hysteria* as an event, a phase in history, and of a subsequent *cure*, an enlightened compromise that was itself an historical event.

Our earliest evidence for the practice of maenadism is the well-known passage from the sixth book of the *Iliad*. There seems to be little scholarly doubt that the Lykourgos here referred to, is in fact the king of the Thracian tribe of Edonians, who were resident in the vicinity of Mt. Pangaion. It is perhaps significant, that while the Lykourgos' tale seems indeed to attest Greek awareness of a specifically Thracian maenadism at least as early as Homer, it seems also to indicate a knowledge as it were from the inside, a connection with the myth-ritual protagonists of some kind;[101] for all other Dionysiac cult-myth belong to the tribes and gene of the Greeks.[102] What the present passage certainly does not do is to provide corroboration for the proponents of the

---

[101] See Marazov, 2000, 31ff. Therefore, the position of the Edonian king as antagonist is pointed out by means ofseveral codes: ethnic(he is Thracian), vegetal(son of tree), animal(he is wolf) and behavioural(he violets all norms).

[102] Peisistratos had connexions of some kind in this area: after his second expulsion it was to this place he retreated to raise money and a mercenary force. This was a half a century before the first Athenian attempt to plant a colony at Amphipolis. Histiaios of Miletos founded a colony called Myrkinos in 510 in the heart of Thrako-Paeonic territory –far from the sea on Lake Prasias, Hdt. 5.11. Pelagonia was a part of Paeonia, and there was a Neleid phratry at Miletos called Pelagonid. Dionysos himself was Dyalos among the Paeonians: Hesych. s.v. Dyalos. And there was an Attic phratry called Dyaleis. Brauron was an Attic deme where Peisistratos had estates, Steph. Byz.q.v. It was an epithet of Artemis and the name of the wife of an Edonian king. Thuc. 4.107.

Thracian origins case: the myth itself (in contradistinction to its literary context) is in all probability of an antiquity comparable to that of most of so-called cult-myths which reveal paradigmatically the perils that lie in store for those who resist or deny Dionysiac divinity incarnate –who *fight against god* (*theomachein*). [103]

It is difficult indeed to draw distinctions between purely literary or apparently literary uses of Dionysiac *theomachia paradeigmata* and ritual uses of the same. For most of examples are set in literary contexts, as is the Homeric example, or in literary works which, however contaminated with ritual content, do not easily come under the rubric of cult documents or even cult literature. The "message" of the cult-myths was an adaptable one: it could serve purely *secular* ends as in the *Iliad* or some much more complicated purpose as in the *Bacchae* where the drama's protagonist is himself the *ritual* offender[104]

(45f.). Here as in the Homeric exemplum the dramatic action is framed by this specially Dionysiac war-cry *theomachein*. The short poem called Λῆναι ἢ Βάκχαι and ascribed to Theokritos ends on the same note.[105] Some have seen in this poem, understandably, a hymn written for performance at a Koan fest of Dionysos Bacchos. And the number of non-mythologized ritual details certainly seem to point in the direction of cult fest. There is one, however, which seem to preclude any other kind of explanation for the poem at a whole.

The Homeric evidence is of particular interest for another reason which is rarely remarked, namely, for the extent of the mythological ramification it quite perspicuously reflects. The divine dive into the Thracian sea must alert us to the fact that there was a whole branch of subaqueous Dionysiaca in existence as early as Homer and probably much earlier.[106] Quintos of Smyrna was a mere imitator, but, predictably, Nonnos shows himself heir to a rich tradition: a varied and fascinating web of underwater wanderings of god and votaries who are quite at home in this wet world.[107] Indeed these *daughters of Ocean* had a place in cult: they too could be called *Nurses of Bacchos*. Mythical tales of a voluntary Dionysiac plunge into the ocean as here or of the throwing of the

---

[103] See Marazov, 2000, 33…It is possible that this Thracian logos reflected some local festivities of the type of *unclean days*, when a ritual king was chosen…merely to take upon himself the sins ot the entire socium and to be expelled from the territory of the kingdom on the very next day. See Вълчинова, 2000, 173-188.

[104] Hos theomachei ta kat' eme kai spondon apo ōthei m'(45ff).

[105] Medeis ton theōn onosaito.

[106] On the *thusthla* and *bouplex* see Burkert, 1985, 198f.; Фол, 1991, 149. Cf. Clem. Al. 2.14 and schol.ad loc.

[107] It is not really necessary to decide whether these lines (Il. 6.129-141) pre-existed as a discreet unit or were composed by the poet; for in the latter case they would reasonably and readily conform to an existing norm.

god into river water vel sim. almost certainly reflect certain ritual acts.[108] And we may plausibly assume that one or more phases of the complex trieteric fest will have featured the ritual act of *katapontismos*.[109] It is tempting, although it lies beyond our present purpose, to speculate about the significance of this ritual act and about *resurrection* and *return* from the sea.[110] It will suffice to have merely called attention here to this obviously important and neglected aspect of our earliest literary evidence for Dionysiac cult practice.

After Homer we find only occasional reference to Thracian Dionysos or to his Thracian votaries until the fifth century when both the *Lykourgos* tetralogy of Aeschylos (as well as a number of plays of Euripides) and the *History* of Herodotos bear witness to Greek knowledge of Thracian orgiastic rites.[111] The title of one of the plays from the *Lykourgeia*, namely, *Bassarai*, shows quite plainly the use of this word as a generic term for the Thracian female votaries of the god. As such it is directly analogous to the Greek Bacchai. But the name Bassarai will in fact have been well known to the Greeks before the time of Aeschylos. For the lyric poet Anakreon must have made rather liberal use of it in his work to judge by the frequency of its occurrence in the exact fragments.

Anakreon was one of the Tean colonists who settled in Thracian Abdera in the mid-sixth century after the Klazomenian venture in the same place. There are in fact mythological adumbrations of *sparagmos* and *omophagia* at Abdera.[112] And the Greek colony lay within the territory of the Thracian tribe of Bistonians whose maenadic practices are reasonably well documented in a much later age primarily in Roman sources. If only because of its proximity to the native tribes who worshipped *Bassareus* then, Anakreon will have had

---

[108] See Hymn. Orph.51.1ff.; cf. ib. 24 to the Nereids. The epithet *chthoniai* in l. 3 of the 51ˢᵗ Hymn is of particular interest in view of Hymn 53 addressed to Amphietes (or the "off-year" Dionysos Bacchos).It is not surprising that there was a separate characterisation of one and the same god according to the different character of the various aspects of the same set of rites. The Lenaion Dionysos was both Euios and Chthonios. Naturally his divine relationships are bound to follow suit.

[109] See Burkert, 1985, 77 and 218-35.

[110] In modern Thracian ritual we hear of the "resurrection" of the dead Kalogeros (one of the ritual protagonists) by his immersion in water; see Kakouri, 1965, 35f; Райчевски, Фол 1993, 95ff.

[111] See Aes. Frg. 69-96 Mette; Eur. Rh. 910-13; cf. Hek. 1267. It is not only the use of the name Bacchos, but the place – Pangaion – which leads us to deduce the connexion between the mantic and the orgiastic rites of Dion. Thrax. Herodotos provides us with one general notice on Thracian Dionysiac worship.

[112] The maenads referred to in this play were of course the *Edonian mothers*. In our late and mostly Latin sources, the generic designation tends to be eschewed in favour of the local, tribal, designation.

reason to know the Thracian name *Bassarai*.[113] But it is of course equally possible that the name belonged to the Greek literary tradition well before the arrival of the Teans on the Thracian coast. Anakreon not only uses the name *Bassarai* vel sim., but he also uses Thracian maenadic metaphor (43Diehl). This is an important piece of evidence; for it enables us to deduce that by the middle of the 6th B.C. the practice of Thracian maenadism was a familiar enough phenomenon to have led the Greek poets to coin a verb, which (in any case, initially) had a specifically Thracian referent, from the generic name for Thracian maenads *Bassarai*. We may in fact plausibly assume that by Anakreon's day this coinage will have been an old one; for we find him using the *maenadic* verb with separate prefix *anabasareō* metaphorically to describe his own, quite literal, intoxication. We may hypothesize then that by the mid-6th century B.C. a range of nominal and verbal *Bassaric* forms – comparable to the Greek *Bacchic* set – were in existence and a part of Greek literary tradition.[114] The verb *anabasareō* may have been a bold innovation of Anakreon; but equally, it may have already belonged to Greek poetic vocabulary. The important thing to note, however, is that this ramification from the generic name *bassarai* presupposes a considerable period of development. According to Marazov(2000, 117):

> *Perhaps it comes from the word signifying their colorful clothes, but it is also probable their coloufulness reflected their limunal unidentified status of women who have left home(the inner space) and have gone out in the mountains (outside in the wilderness) in order to celebrate the orgies of their deity.*

Similarly, the lavish exploitation of *Bacchic* metaphor we find in the 5th century B.C. presupposes a slow linguistic development of which the accidents of transmission have not even left us faint traces. One of our earliest example is also one of the boldest.[32] Maenadic metaphor had a long life, beginning with Homer and surviving well into the Christian era.[115] In the pages of Nonnos we witness the derailment of Bacchic metaphor largely because of this author's exuberant excesses – one might almost say – because of the utter *maenadissation* of Anacreon has more references to Dionysos than any other poet of his or

---

[113] The god too is called *Bassareus*. Cf. Schl. Lyc. 771. 1343: *Bassara* is the same like alopex, the well-known Thracian headdress of fox-furs.

[114] E.g. *katabassareō* which is not found in our source material, although it is a distinct analogical possibility on the basis of *katabakchiousthe*, Eur. Ba. 109; cf. *anabakcheuō*, ib. 864.

[115] The word *mainas* first occurs in a short comparison at Il. 22.460 to describe the distraught Andromache. Cf. ib. 6.388f. Cf. Hymn Dem. 386 which is the first literary reference to the familiar maenadic mountain stage.

previous age. It is clear that Anacreon refer to a purely Thracian phenomen. There must have been a strong tendency in Greece to domesticate Dionysos. The Greeks who came to Thrace were confronted with the original cult. The process of Greek colonization and cult realities in Abdera is summarized by Isaac so: [116]

> *It can therefore be said that the numerous references to Dionysos and his cult in the extant work of Anacreon, as well as the position of this god in Abdera reflect an interest raised by contact with Thracian culture. This in turn shows that there must have been a mutual exchange of ideas even in the earliest stages of colonization, when Greeks snd Thracianns were fighting each other for possession of the site. It is clear that the foundation of Greek colonies, led to intimate relations between Greeks and Thracians at all levels of society. This must have been an important cause in a process in a process of mental acculturation, especially in the colonies themselves.*

There is one further point we might consider in connection with Thracian *Bassarai*. It is a generic one: It seems that apparently Thracian Dionysiac names occur rather often in poems with Dionysiac subject matter which belong to the category of *anathemata* or dedications. The focus in these for the most part short poems is on maenadic realia not maenadic activity: the concrete physical objects of maenadic work and play, the fawnskin, thyrsos, torch, etc. of course do find a place in the *oreibasic* material – the descriptive portrayals of maenadic activities *in the mountains*; but the focus there is on the action. The static dedicatory poems on the other hand derive their *action* if at all, from the objects themselves. But there is one object which occurs sometimes in the latter, and never in the former. It is the *liknon*. The following epigram[117] consists in large part of a rather lifeless, list of maenadic ritual particulars; its *raison d'être* must have been audience knowledge of and interest in these realia. This text raises interesting questions and not a few difficulties. The author, Phalaikos, may have been a Thracian; but the reference to the *Bassaric* thiasos could also be merely Thracian colouring. First, it obviously does not belong to the genre we are considering here, although the relevant lines are otherwise

---

[116] See Isaac, 1986, 82ff.

[117] Strepton Bassarikou rombon thiasoio myopa
  Kai skylos amfidromou stikton ahaïineō
  Kai korybanteiōn iahēmata kōnoforou kamaka
  Kai thyrsou hloeron kōnoforou kamaka
  Kai koufaio baryn tympanon bromon ēde forethen
  Pollaki mitrodetou liknon hyperthe komēs
  Euanthe Bakhō tēn entromon hanika thyrsois
  Atromon eis proposeis heira megemfiasa.

unparalleled in Greek or Latin poetry. Euanthe's dedications to her god are copious; but it is perhaps significant that the last named item in her list is the *liknon* – an object of especial awe as we shall see below. It is in this generic context then that we can perhaps better understand Agaue's now sober prayer at the end of *Bacchae* (1383–87). Her concluding words serve to set the *dedication* and the preceding mythopoiesis in the recurrent and real performance of, as it were here, universal Bacchic ritual. In turn we may reasonably deduce from these lines that the Bacchic species of *anathemata* will have been well established by the 5th century B.C. It follows therefore that the assignment of Anakreon's epigram[118] is certainly a plausible one.[119] The names are perhaps best described as Thrako-Greek, although there are no overly Thracian indicators like *Bassaris*. Moreover, if the 6th century B.C. was the period during which the genre became established or somehow fixed, this fact would help to explain the apparently disproportionately high number of Thracian names or elements in it at much later dates. For this was the period when Thracian maenads captured the imagination of the Greek poets. In the classical period and, perhaps surprisingly, in the Hellenistic age as well, when Greek poets wrote about the mountaining-dancing of the female votaries of Dionysos Bacchos, it was Greek maenads in Greek mountains they described. Not until the Augustan period in the works of the Roman poets would the Dionysiac literary focus shift back to Thrace.

In his *Life of Alexander* Plutarch provides us with a notice of considerable importance which attests not only the maenadic practices of real Macedonian women who were called Mimallones and Klodones,[120] but also those of Thracian Edonian women, who are perhaps best known to us from myth, and of – "the Thracians of the Haimos". Here, however, it is not so much the tribes themselves or the comparison, that will concern, but rather the ritual particulars – the likna, the snakes and not least, the presence of men (Alex, 2).

By Alexander's time much of southern Thrace was nominally Macedonian; there were tribes which had mingled in previous centuries on the northern borders of Macedon with Thracian and Thrako-Paeonic tribes: Paeonians, Mygdonians, Illyrians, Dardanians and still others.[121] Macedon's rulers needed and exploited Thracian mines. Interest in her northern and western neighbors

---

[118] A.P. 6.134; cf. Eur. Ba. 1169ff. and A.P. 6.172, 6.74.

[119] Agē dē fer hemin ō pai
    kelebēn, okōs amystin
    prōpio. Ta men dek' enkeas
    hydatos. Ta men pente d'oinou
    kyatos ōs anybristi ana dēute bassarēsō.

[120] On Mimallones and Kiodones see Polyain. 4.1; Strab.468; Athen. 5.198E.

[121] See Делев, 2014.

will have been great, and information will have kept pace with the demand for it. As we have seen above, the Greeks were familiar with the Thracian Edonians at least as early as Homer and probably much earlier. And there were colonies planted very early on the south Thracian coast. But the tribes of the Haimos and their customs cannot have been known to many. What then were Plutarch's sources? We in fact know that he used a great number for his *Life of Alexander*; but it is specifically his possible source for the maenadism of the Thracians of the Haimos that must concern us. Ptolemy Soter, one of Alexander's ablest commanders and later king of Egypt, we know accompanied him on his Thracian campaign;[122] Strabo in fact uses him as a source, and even his brief discussion shows that Ptolemy in the best Hellenistic tradition took some interest in ethnography.[123] Ptolemy is therefore almost certain to have been Plutarch's source or one of them, for the comparison of Macedonian and Haemonian *maenads*. For Plutarch *to threskeuein* seems to be synonymous with emotional excesses in religious performance. But in a late lexicographer we find a gloss which may enable us to be a bit more specific about the immediate cause – or one of them – of this Dionysiac extasy: *liknostefei. liknon stefoumenos. threskeuei*.[124] From this notice we may plausibly conclude that the wreathing of the *liknon* was a particularly ecstatic point in the ritual ceremonies. Indeed the contents of the liknon (and *kista*)[125] were objects of veneration and awe; they were things which could not be spoken about or revealed to the uninitiated[126]. The contents themselves could be called *mysteria*;[127] or the container, as here, could be called *mystic*. If then we are to assume that Plutarch was using Hellenistic sources for this part of his *Life* – Ptolemy Soter or a source dependent on him – the account before us is indeed one of our earliest notices attesting the use of *likna* in Dionysiac orgiastic ritual. Even earlier, however, is Demosthenes' description of the role played by Aeschines in the orgiastic cult of Sabazios where among other things he is said to have been a liknon-bearer

---

[122] Plut. Alex. 16.

[123] E.g. schol. ad Eur. Alk. 968 (II 239, 10 Schw.) = Kern, OF, tost. 37; cf. ib. 40.

[124] Hesych. q.v.

[125] It is tolerably clear that there were at least two kinds of basket used in the bacchic rites – kistai and likna. It is also fairly clear that there is occasional confusion in source material, i.e. the kista appears to have been used sometimes as generic designation which will have included or indicated likna. For it is almost certain that the *orgion arrheton* of Dionysos Bacchos belongs to the liknon and not to the *kista*. On the other hand we cannot state categorically that the term liknon was never used as a generic rubric under which kistai were subsumed.

[126] See e.g. Clem. Al. Protr. 2.19; Val. Fl. 2.267: *plenas tacita formidine cistas*; Cat. 64.259. In Apul. Met. 11.27 a priest of Osiris – Dion.'s familiar Egyptian counterpart, carries *thyrsos, hederas et tacenda quaedam*. See Marazov, 2000, 211.

[127] See Henrichs, 1969, 228f.

(*liknoforos*).[128] The fact that this particular title does not appear until the Roman age among the elaborate lists of Dionysiac cult functionaries, for example, in the well-known Agripinnilla inscription, of course proves nothing. For we have no comparable Dionysiac inscriptions from the classical period, attesting such functional ramification and hierarchical structure in the *bacchica* of that age.[129] From the Hellenistic age too we have a mere handful of inscriptions pertaining to orgiastic Dionysiac religion, and none of these travel to anywhere near the same extent in this sacral discourse, although there are ample indications of hierarchy and ramification. All the elements, however, or most of them – the thyrsos, krater, torch, milk, etc. – are known to as one way or another from classical and earlier sources; they were used and significant in Dionysiac orgiastic ritual. What is new is the penchant for inscribing these uses or offices on stone. But it seems in any case almost certain that this particular cult title – *liknophoros* – was known to Demosthenes' audience, whoever we take Sabazios to be, first and foremost as belonging to the orgiastic cult of Dionysos. M.P. Nilsson in his work devoted a great deal of his attention to the subject of the *liknon* in the cult of Dionysos, its history and use. It is noteworthy that in his discussion of the *liknon* in early times he rejects out of hand the Plutarch passage quoted above finding "very suspect". His reasons are not convincing: "It is embroidered with well-known *clichés*. Elsewhere there is no mention of snakes in the *liknon*, only in the *cista mystica*. First, to claim that the passage is "embroidered with well-known clicheés" seems to involve a *petitio principi* as well as another error in logic; for if the *liknon* (with or without snakes) was a Dionysiac clicheé in the 4th century B.C. then it will necessarily have been a significant Dionysiac "symbol" in previous centuries. But Nilsson argues that the *liknon* became a symbol of the *Bacchic mysteries* only in the Hellenistic age. As to his claim that elsewhere there is no mention of snakes in the *liknon* he himself later in his discussion provides the evidence of its erroneousness. [130] Finally, the presence of men, far from convicting Plutarch or his source of fabrication or playful elaboration should alert us to the possibility that what we have here described is simply another phase of trieteric orgiastic activity.

The *Arretine vases* of the Roman age, which perpetuate Greek motifs and which we can trace back directly to the low-relief clay and metal bowls of the Hellenistic period, show scenes of Bacchic initiation in which both men and

---

[128] De cor. 18. 259.

[129] If in fact the terminology existed in 4th C Athens, it makes no sense to think of it as having been devised ad hoc: for the advent of a foreign god. Besides, if Strabo took this passage as a reference to Sabazia as something sui generis, there were others who did not; see e.g. Plut. Mor. 671F; Harpokr.s.v.

[130] Nilsson in fact devotes some three pages to a discussion of the relevant *Orphic* fragment, 42ff.

women participate.[131] Here and on other related monuments of the same period the *liknon* is prominent and its significance perspicuous. It is carried on the heads of women, and in the hands of Silenos; it is also carried on the veiled head of the neophyte or held above his head.

A stucco relief from the Villa Farnesina shows the revelation of the phallos in the *liknon* to a young boy; and the great fresco in the Villa dei Misteri in Pompeii and a mosaic from Cuicul show a woman unveiling the *liknon* with one hand and with the other grasping the revealed phallos it contains. It is abundantly clear from these examples, all of which probably and most of which certainly, derive from Hellenistic models, that the veiling and the unveiling of the *liknon* was an integral feature of orgiastic Dionysiac ritual and that the revelation of the *phallos* was significant not only for the women votaries of the god, but also for men and boys. Furthermore it is clear that the *phallos* in the *liknon* was not only a *sacred symbol*, it was *cult object* of the greatest importance in the initiation ceremonies of the cult of Dionysos Bacchos. It is therefore virtually unthinkable that such an integral feature of Bacchic telestic ritual was once of less prominence in cult or, indeed, non-existent. Yet both the monuments and our literary texts before the Hellenistic age are strangely silent.

There are two points to be made which will explain this apparent anomaly. The first can be mentioned here only in passing: once we have established the category and, indeed, the reality of the *mixed feast* of *bacchai* and satyrs (men got up in a certain fixed and prescribed was) as one of the phases of the trieteric-orgiastic festival complex, then we extend the range of our archaeological evidence back to the Archaic age. But we must in turn account for the absence of the *liknon* itself in these *mixed* festival scenes before the Hellenistic age. We know that the contents of both the *cista mystica* and the mystic *liknon* were neither to be revealed to the eyes of the profane nor spoken about to those who had not *been shown* themselves. They were *aporrheta*.

Ritual convention is constant; artistic conventions and the conventions of society in general change with the passage of time. The conventions of Minoan-Mycenaean art, for example, proscribed obscene representations of any kind. Classical and archaic vase painters, on the other hand, seem at times obsessed with ithyphallic satyrs. But the artists of the Hellenistic age, who portrayed scenes of the *mixed festival* of satyrs and bacchai, to judge from the Arretine vases and other Roman derivatives, turned their attention elsewhere: Hellenistic artists freed by the conventions of their own craft, broke also with

---

[131] See Nilsson 89ff. He remarks that: *As usual the representation is transferred onto the mythical plane, with Satyrs and Silenus appearing instead of men.* But Satyrs and Seilenoi are men dressed up in a particular kind of costume for the trieteric-orgiastic feast. This is the significance of Plutarch's reference to *andres* at Alex. 2.

the pagan tradition which respected the proscriptions of the mystery cults, and dragged the hidden and unmentionable objects into the bright light of day for the eyes of posterity, as chance would have it, as well as for the viewing of their own contemporaries. Later, the Christians took particular pleasure in these revelations. Horace, however, observed pagan propriety, and refused to mention the *unmentionable*. How widespread the open disregard was, we cannot tell. We happen to know, however, that at the Dionysiac feast of the *Katagogia* at Ephesos as late as the Imperial period men masqueraded in processions wearing both masks and certain *unseemly attachments* which must have included *phalloi* – and probably *tails* as well. Thus our art-historical evidence, if we are not fully cognizant of changes in artistic conventions – or certainly of the fact that there is change, can seriously mislead us.

We must continually remind ourselves that we are dealing with a festival of vast proportions and many phases. In this context Diodoros provided us with some useful information. For he tells us that the Greeks honored the *phallos* in the Dionysiac orgies and fests in both the mysteries and the initiatory rites and sacrifices of Dionysos.[132] There were segregated feasts of men and those of women; the former we know took place indoors, the latter in open air. And there was a *mixed* feast which took place for the most part outdoors to judge from both literary sources and the monuments, but may have included an indoor phase as well; but here the evidence is very scanty. There were at least this number of phases belonging to the trieteric-orgiastic festival complex. It lies beyond our present purpose to endeavor to distinguish between *mysteries* and *initiatory rites*. For one thing the terms *mysteria*, *teletai* and *orgia* were too often used interchangeably. As we have seen above in an Hellenistic epigram the female votary of the god carried the *liknon* on her mitre-bound head; the Roman Arretine vases confirm this view as does this testimony of Proklos.[133]

The significance of this notice of course hinges entirely upon the meaning of the rare word *kradiaios*. Nilsson follows LSJ in interpreting it to mean *belonging to the heart* as if derived from the Doric form for *heart kradia* in spite of the fact that no comparable adjectival form exists for *kradia*. But if the negative philological evidence in itself is not persuasive, perhaps we can see by example that *kradiaios* means what we should expect it mean, namely, *made of fig wood* which is in fact how LSJ translate here. How then to interpret this

---

[132] timan touto to morion en tois mystērios
kai tais tou theou touto teletais te
kai thysiais…
[133] in Plat. Timaeum, i, p. 407 Diehl = Kern, OF fr. 199. Here Hipta puts a liknon on her head and surrounds it with a serpent. liknon epi tēs kefalēs themenē kai drakonti auto peristefasa to(n) kradioion hypodehetai Dionyson.

epithet applied to the god is of course another question. The possibilities seem obvious: first, the reference could be to a wooden (fig wood) image of the god. Second, it could be a reference to the *morion tou theou* made of fig wood.[134] The Christian Clement can perhaps throw some light here. He ingeniously combines an explanation for the *origin* of the *phalloi* which are so prominent in the Dionysiac rites with Herakleitos' equation of Dionysos and Hades:

> *... Cutting off a branch from a fig-tree which was at hand, he shaped it into likeness of a phallos, and then made a show of keeping his promise to the dead man.*[135]

This is aetiology; but it explains not the procession of the *phallos* at certain Dionysiac festivals, but the existence of numerous small, or as it were, life-size, *phalloi* and their *display* at a particular feast, during which groups of men got themselves up at satyrs with phallic attachments, and which we can also identify from Herakleitos as occurring during the month of Lenaion. This interpretation seems to accord much better with both our archaeological and literary evidence. Unlike Plutarch, who was himself initiated into the Dionysiac mysteries, and therefore sworn to an oath of silence, Clement feels duty bound to divulge the contents in order to hold them up to the ridicule he thinks they deserve. Elsewhere he speaks of *kista* and *aideia* (78, 79). Now if in fact the *phallos* was, as we are constantly reminded in our ancient sources, *aporrēton ti* then the need for euphemism and periphrasis when dealing with it in words is self-evident – and all the more so of course to the extent that *phallos* was held to be the *morion tou theou*. Thus we hear of the *arousing* or *awakening* of Liknites at Delphi, i.e. the god in this particular aspect.[80] And, interestingly, the activity is correlated with an *aporretos thysia*.[81] The 52nd*Orphic Hymn* to Trieterikos in fact calls the god *orgion arrēton*. along with a long list of his mostly more familiar epithets.[82] And when Clement refers to the *orgion Dionysou Bassarou* the epithet *Bassaros*, which is properly Thracian and doubtless in his source, may plausibly be seen as having a certain distancing effect because of its Thracian colouring; it is then partially analogous to the device of euphemism. The *phallos* of the sacrificial animal was a symbol of fertility; its procurement in the formal sacrificial ceremonies of the Trieterides will have signaled the end of the symbolic period of *akarpia*. For *akarpia* was the *nosos Dionysiacos*–infertility of humans, animals and fields. This was obviously a *ritual fiction*; for nature has never observed a biennial rhythm of want and plenty. This is perhaps most perspicuous in the complex of Lykourgos myth, which, at least in the synopsis transmitted by Ps. Apollodoros, preserves

---

[134] Cf. Diod. I 22. 6f. and Clem. Al. Protr. 2.19.
[135] Protr. 2.30.

this particular myth-ritual aspect as well as the *sparagmos* – in this case by the animal transform of the maenads, (3.5.7). It is tempting indeed to see in the two major bodies of Theban myth – Oidipous saga and Dionysiac *cult-myth* – a complicated bifurcation, i.e., a separate development and characterisation of the *nosos Dionysiakos* which in Lykourgos myth is still integral. Incest, plague and famine at Thebes belong to the Oidipous cycle which is *prima facie* unrelated to the Pentheus cycle. The cult hymn of the women of Elis, which Plutarch preserves, enables us in turn to connect the *healing foot* with the trieteric animal sacrifice and castration. There is an analogous instance of such euphemism in art historical evidence, which belongs roughly to the same period as Sophokles' hymn. A great deal has been said about the so-called *Vlasto Chous*, which, in spite of its shape, is most plausibly assigned because of the representation it shows, to the festival of the Lenaia. There are a number of points of interest in connection with this vase; here, however, we must restrict ourselves to one – the significance of the bearded prosopon of the god lying in the *liknon*. In this case there can be no doubt whatsoever about the association of ideas. The adjustment is not an easy one when we are presented with the head, as it were, in the flesh, instead of the *phallos*, which as *aporrheton ti* could not be shown or talked about to the profane. In the case of the two kletic hymns quoted above what we seem to have is the god (the whole of him) conceptualised as anthropomorphic, and the part – the *phallos* – conceptualised now as animal and now as human. In each hymn the part receives equal attention to the whole. We cannot here speculate about the significance of this great variety of *phalloi* or be more specific about their use; but we have seen evidence enough to refute Farnell's dictum that:

> *In spite of the prevalence of his phallic ritual Dionysos was not generally recognised in Hellas as the divine source of human or animal procreation.*

The tribes and places we will now consider were accorded a prominent place in the Dionysiac literary tradition; but it should be made clear at the outset that there is independent evidence from a variety of prose authors which seems to confirm the picture of Thracian maenadism the poets have bequeathed us. As we shall see, the majority of notices are drawn from the works of the Roman poets – mostly Augustans, though some come from their successors. For the most part the references are *contemporary* in character, not mythological. In the works of the Roman poets the generic term for Thracian maenads, *Bassarai*, begins to give way to the local and tribal designations: Edones, Ismariae, nurus Ciconum, Haemoniae matres, although certainly Bassarai are still to be found. The Greek poets when referring to their own or to Thracian maenads for the most part used Greek generic names: *mainas*, *bacche* and less often, *thyias*. Naturally in hymnic *amplificatio* these maenads tended to acquire local names if the cult seat was not otherwise designated.[136] After Anakreon in non-mythological contexts the Greek poets seem to have given up the use of the term *Bassarai* with the single generic exception we have noted above, namely, in the *anathemata*.

Roman strategists had criss-crossed Thrace on their campaigns; Dalmatia and Pannonia were by the time of the early Empire *household words* in Rome due largely to the successful efforts of Tiberius and Drusus. And Tomis on the Pontos Euxeinos coast had become the backyard dumping ground for the state's undesirables – those who would corrupt the good manners of Augustin society Ovid was certainly more antiquarian than he was anthropologist. He might have told us much; what he did in fact leave us from the years of his exile is some of his least attractive poetry and very little ethnography.[137] He does, however, provide us with one of those relatively rare notices which attests the practice of maenadism for Thrace in general rather than for a particular tribe or place.[138] At first glance this seems to be but another one among countless portraits of distraught women with streaming hair who are compared to the female votaries of Dionysos. These, though sometimes staid and somber on the myriad pots that will have lined Roman as well as Greek cellar shelves, to the mind's eye are never still. They are always dishevelled, sometimes distressed by the marauding hands of satyrs, sometimes enraptured by the nearness of their god. The Roman poets in fact show a certain predilection for the flying locks and the peculiar carriage of the head. But this does nothing to controvert Dodds' apt picture of the compartmentalisation to which the Romans subjected the Greek god and his unruly crew. It should not cause surprise that these *functionalists* show such a well-defined penchant for conventionalised disorder. And it is of interest that, conversely, in the Greek poets this *manic* aspect of maenadic behaviour, summarised as it were by the *fusis capillis*, is by no means to the fore, though it is very common indeed on the vases. There is, however, another point we ought to note: while the maenadic similes are common enough at all times – beginning with Homer – the additional prosaic tag, which Ovid gives to remind us that he is indeed describing a phenomenon from *real life*, is exceptional. In fact the maenad simile by Ovid's day will have been so highly conventional that it might well be felt necessary to underline the *reality* of these Thracians, to make them indeed realer than the

---

[136] Entha Kōrykiai steihousi Nymfai Bakhides.

[137] See Gandeva, 1978, 103-109.

[138] Mentis inops rapitur quails audire solemus
Threicias fusis Maenadas ire comis. (F. 4.457f.)

maenads of countless other similes, to make them topical as well as typical. It is certainly very likely that Ovid's contemporaries in Rome did indeed hear a great deal about Thracian maenads in action. Pliny, for example had heard or knew a current report about the Thracian *sacra Liberi patris*. Pliny's et nunc must remove any doubt about the flow of information into Rome from Romans in the Thracian field.

We may turn now to the individual tribes and tribal centres of the Thracians which were well known as places of maenadic activity. It perhaps make some sense to begin with the more remote, namely, the maenadism of the Haimos region for we have already considered in passing Plutarch's possible sources. As is well known the Haimos mountains transect Thrace more or less across her centre from her western border to the Euxine. To the south lay the Thracian plain, to the north, the flatlands that stretched to the Ister (Danube). Beyond the Ister lay the Getic desert and the wastes of Skythia. The Greeks knew the Thracian litoral well; but her interiors did not invite this widely colonization race. Thrace was opened up by the Romans, and they stayed on. The country was incorporated into the Empire, divided into fifty commands and troops were quartered. The Greeks of the coastal cities from the Haimos to the Ister knew the Thracian Getai; and the same tribe were known in Athens as slaves. They were a huge tribe and difficult to pin down geographically. But they were at home on the northern slopes of the Haimos and in the deserts beyond the Ister which bore their name. It is therefore quite likely that Plutarch's *Thracian women of Haimos* will have included Getic women. Occasionally the Getai are specified in our Dionysiac notices for this region; but in most cases we must simply resort to guesswork. For the area involved is so vast and the tribes so numerous that the loose designation *hai peri ton Haimon Thrēssai* could include some or most of the following tribes: Triballi, Bessi, Krobizi, Koralli, Moisi or Mysi, the Maidi or Medi, the Agathyrsi and many others in addition to the Getai.[139] But these tribes, apart from the Getai (and these not to any great extent) do not belong to the Dionysiac literary tradition, though we must suspect that many of them were indeed practitioners of the trieteric-orgiastic rites of the god. Pomponius Mela numbers Haimos among the Dionysiac mountains of Thrace.[140] The inclusion of Mt. Obrelos in his list makes us suspect that Pomponius is using non-poetic sources; for this mountain certainly does not belong to the Thracian Dionysiac literary tradition. Valerius Flaccus(II, 537) too lists the

---

[139] See Фол, 1975, 60ff.

[140] montis interior (sc. Thracia) adtollit Haemon et Rhodopen et Oberlon sacris Liberi patris et coetu Maenad um primum Orpheo celebratos initiante (Pomp. Mela, De chorogr., 2.1.1.)

Haimos as one of the Thracian mountains that "groan" with Dionysiac madness. And Horace(Od. XII), like Pomponius, knows that Orpheus belongs to these mountains. Vergil singles out the Getai from the Haimos tribes who along with *universal (Thracian) nature* lamented the death of Orpheus.[141] Finally, the notice of Statius(Silv. III. 3. 169) is one of the few poetical references we have to the *Trieterides* in the comprehensive sense (in contradiction to merely the maenadic phase of trieteric activity) in Thrace. For it attests male orgiastic activity for the Getai of Haimos, while we can easily supply the maenadic from other sources. In addition, it is our only source which attests the biennial rhythm of the orgia specifically for this region in the temporal phrase: *geminae iam sidere brumae –at the (time of) star of the twin (second) winter*. Statius has made the god himself *archegete* (instead of the usual "Orpheus") of his own rites from which we may plausibly deduce that he was following a different tradition from Vergil and Pomponius. The following notice too contains an undifferentiated reference to *orgia* in the Haimos region. But it is of considerable interest; for it brings directly into the main-line orgiastic religion of Dionysos Thrax, Aristaios, who is elsewhere an ancillary figure in Dionysiac myth.[142] Diodoros in elating the impressive history of Aristaios begins with his Libyan birth. He goes on to connect him with Beotia, Keos, Sicily and vicinity. Finally, as the account goes, Aristaios went north to Thrace to Dionysos, participated in the *orgia* and became a disciple of the god from whom he learnt many useful things. When he had dwelt for some time in the vicinity of Haimos, he disappeared; and he received honors not only there among the barbaroi, but also among the Greeks. Why was the Haimos region singled out from among the numerous Thracian possibilities as the place of Aristaios' final residence? Or indeed why was he connected with this area at all? There is in fact a plausible explanation. On the summit of the huge ridge of Haimos where it projects into the sea, there was a town called Aristaeum.[143] This is particular interest in connection with well-known *autor* of the *Arimaspeia* who was also a metic in many places. This Aristaios was a native of Prokonnesos where there was also a town called Aristaeum – reputedly a colony of Miletos. Scholars take this Aristaios for flesh and blood, but do not connect him with or mention his Cyrenian namesake although he too had gone north at Apollo's request and he too was connected with southern Italy (Metapontum). Our evidence suggests that this area was indeed a centre of *Bacchic learning*: somewhere high in the Haimos

---

[141] In the fourth Georgic(4.461-63) affiliation of Orpheus is alluded by numerous geographical and mythical references to Thrace.

[142] See Лазова 2001; Ustinova 2002, 267-288; Jordanova 2016

[143] Plin. 4.18.

mountains there was a temple of Dionysos[144] (and perhaps an oracle as well) which was said to contain certain *anagraphai* of Orpheus on wooden tablets. It is of course tempting to connect these notices with the previous one, but there can be no certainty. The tradition of the wooden tablets is, however, an old one. And a reliable source connected these with the god Dionysos and the Haimos mountains in the 4th century B.C. There are of course Dionysiac parallels closer to home. And Guthrie interestingly compares the bronze tablets which were said to have been brought to Delos by two seers from the land of the Hyperboreans on which was written an account of the soul in Hades. But is by no means clear that such *anagraphai* would contain material of an eschatological or mystical nature. For the word has a decidedly legalistic ring: it occurs in fact in a quasi-technical sense in a late Bacchic cult inscription from Imperial Athens.Unfortunately it is not possible here to pursue the ever enticing Orphic or Orpheus question, or the interesting and certainly related question of Thracian *literacy* (*sophia*) about which there was lively controversy at least as early as the 4th century B.C. But we easily deduce that the Haimos was an important centre of trieteric-orgiastic Dionysiac worship in Thrace, that this complex of worship was of considerable antiquity and that to the local Thracian cult of the god belonged not only the familiar *orgia* but also, in some sense, a *theology*.[145]

The Sithonians occupied the middle prong of the Thracian Chalkidike[146], and the country still bears their name. Our notices on Dionysiac religion in this area are relatively few in number. In fact Ovid[147] give us only notice on Sithonian maenadism. His information is set within a literary device of which the Roman poets were particularly fond –the *falsa baccheia*: the imagined trieteric festival *mise en scene* for the mythical action. The regular and recurrent ritual feast is thus projected back to a time contemporary with the supposed event. The main point to note in this passage is that the Sithonian women seem to have by-passed not only their own small local mountains, but also Pangaion on their way to Rhodope. This means, if Ovid has got his information right, that they will have joined some group of local women for their *oreibasia*. Such examples of maenadic *theoria* are not unparalleled in Greece or elsewhere in Thrace as we shall see below.We may be reasonably certain that there were branches of Sithones or related clans in other parts of Thrace: We hear of Sithon who was king of the tribe of Odomanti; the latter were resident in classical times round Pangaion, chiefly to the north. And

---

[144] See Фол, 1989, 71-80; 2002, 210ff; Boteva 1997, 287-298.
[145] See Фол, 1986.
[146] See Делев, 2014
[147] Ovid., Meth., 587-600.

Pliny put Sithones very far afield indeed. This is not at all surprising given the diffusion patterns of Thracian tribes. Strabo in fact calls the Sithones a tribe of Edonians – a plausible ascription since we know that the Edonians and Odomanti were related. Finally we know that there were once Edonians in the foothills of Rodope in the vicinity of Krenides. And all of these facts support Ovid's assertion.

Horace provides us with one of the few remaining notices on the Sithonian connection with the god. And Kadmos, as we have already noted above, was associated with the region of Thrace: a tradition preserved by the immense eclecticism of Nonnos makes Harmonia his wife a Sithonian – interesting among other reasons because of the obvious comparison of the names Sithones and Sidones.[115]

After the tribe of Edonii who had a Dionysiac fame that extended to myth as well as cult, the Bistonians are perhaps the most often mentioned of the Thracian tribes both Greek and Roman poets as practitioners of maenadic rites. In fact the name Bistones was sometimes used to indicate *Thracian* because it was so common. The tribe inhabited the area round Abdera and Dikaia. Something has already been said about Bistonian maenads as possible models for the 6th century poet Anakreon, who was a Tean colonist at Abdera, and about the man-eating mares of Diomedes. The evidence which follows is almost exclusively maenadic. But it is important to note that there are two categories: notices which attest the maenadism of the Bistonian women without designating the place of the company and notices which indicate that these women travelled to the greatly distant Ismaros to join the local Kikonian women *eis oros*. This is of course of especial interest and significance in view of the *theoria* of Athenian women to Delphi, where they joined the local Delphians "in the mountains" at the biennial rites. There are two completely independent places of information, which invite us to lend credence to our poetic sources: It appears, that the Kikones and the Bistones were in fact related tribes, or clans of the same tribe – in any case, that they has close ties of kinship. Tradition also united them by making Oiagros' son Orpheus, once their common ruler. There are a number of references to Orpheus among the Bistonians; some of these tell of his death at the hands of the local women. The Hellenistic poet Phanokles does not call the murderous maenads; in his account they are irate wives, whose husbands have been led away from them by the man responsible for Thracian homosexuality. The anonymous author of the next notice is kinder to Bistonians: these too are tattooed on arms, which are rent in grief for the dead Orpheus. There is no overt sign, that these mourning women were responsible for his death; they are part of lamenting *universal nature*. Maenads can also be compared to other maenads; Statius compared the Theban *mothers* to their northern, Bistonian counterparts.[148] Valerius Flaccus[149] gives us a rather confused assemblage. Horace too mentions Bistonian maenads by name.[150] The *iugis separatis* are certainly a reference to the *oreibasia*; the following notice again from Horace will enable us to assign to the mountain its probable name. This is a complex poem. Here, however, we can consider only one or two points, which have a direct bearing on Thracian maenadism. First, however, a brief sketch might be in order; for in Dionysiac terms the poem is more complex, than meets the eye. Horace imagines himself as a male reveller and votary of Dionysos Bacchos sacred to the god. And it is in this imagined context that he singles himself out from the Dionysiac plurality. For the context of the Roman's poet's *philetimia* is private; the Greek poet's is public. In lines 14 ff. he returns himself to the plurality: to *follow the god* (*sequi deum*) is to *go in a thiasos* by definition. The poem then reflects divisions: the complicated nexus of private and public roles of the poet, who has chosen to sing the *cecus egregii Caesaris*. Horace has given us in very abbreviated form all the necessary Dionysiac makers: the season, *nive candidam Thracen*; the time, *exsomnis* expresses somewhat elliptically the *all-night festival* of the maenads; the place, *in iugis*, (*Rhodopen lustratam*). Unlike most poets who wrote about Thracian maenads and their mountains Horace had actually seen Pangaion and Rhodope. It is unlikely that he will have seen the Hebros: it is a long way from Philippi; but a few miles east of Philippi he would have seen Rhodope rise to a not very impressive grandeur, and to the west across the plain the lone Pangaion. It was here he *changed his fait* in the autumn of 43. It is to this place then that his thoughts return in his ode to Pompeius, his friend and then fellow Republican:

> *O saepe mecum tempus in ultimum / deducte Bruto militia duce… / tecum Philippos et celerem fugam / sensi relicta non bene parmula /(Od. II. 7) …*

He ends the poem with an oblique reference to the mountain that they both will have seen every day during the protracted struggles of that campaign: *non ego sanius / bacchabor Edonis: recepto / dulce mihi furere est amico.* As an Edonian maenad *raves madly* when her god *returns* so Horace will find it *sweet to rave now that his friend has returned.*

When Horace thought of Philippi, he thought of Pangaion, not Rhodope. It is this southern spur or a part of it that was called in antiquity Mt. Ismaros. Here was a vigorous centre of maenadic activity. It is from the peaks of the southern spur that the Hebros could be seen, or at least one could imagine it being seen; for it flows to the sea skirting the eastern base of this spur. Here

---

[148] (Theb. 80-85)
[149] (Arg., I, 726ff)
[150] (Od. III, 25)

according to our evidence Bistonian women will have come to participate in a joint *oreibasia* with the local Kikonian women every second year. The two poetic notices we have on Bistonian *theoria* look very much like reflecting the same tradition:

Vergil like Phanokles has made uxorial jealousy the cause of Orpheus traditional Dionysiac death. This is in effect but a variation on the *falsa baccheia*, the ritual setting for the mythical event whose real cause is *ouden pros ton Dionyson* and serves to remind us that maenads are after all really quite *normal*.[151] Ovid has combined other traditional Orphic details with the maenadic death. The next notic is apparently *contemporary* in character, i.e. non-mythological.[152] Thus we have at Ismaros-Maroneia a pattern of worship which bears comparison with that at Delphi: biennial maenadic rites on the near-by Mt. Ismaros, and, if we are to believe our sources, a visit in each place to a cave for some purpose; in addition we have maenadic theoria attested for Bistonian women at Ismaros and for Athenian women at Delphi; for Delphi we have a winter date for the *Trieteris*, at Ismaros we have poetic evidence of the same. Here, we must consider that the generic *pull* in bacchic or maenadic scenes is towards *green*: Although *snowy* vel sim. is indeed an *ornamental epithet* of Thrace, in this case the *cold caves* may well be an example of meteorological realism. It would be wrong, however, to press this point. For, while the biennial periodicity was indeed an unvarying feature of *baccheia*, a winter date, in all probability, was not, although it was certainly the most common.

Which are the centers of Thracian menadism? First, a word about the Kikonians themselves. The earliest mention we have of them is in the Catalogue(Il., II, 844-850): they are allies of the Trojans, their leader is Euphemos the son of Keades.[153] They, like the Paionians, are given a separate status instead of being subsumed under the rubric, Thracians. One reason for this positive discrimination could well have been their "advanced" civilization: the size and sophistication of their archaeological remains are impressive and date to the Bronze Age. We also have evidence from myth which suggests early connexions between Athens and Ismaros.

In the Catalogue we have seen that the Kikonians were ranked as allies of the Trojans and classed as a separate *people*; in later sources, however, they are but another one of scores of Thracian tribes: their day of glory was in the distant past, their fame had wanes and their territory had shrunk considerably by

---

[151] (G. IV, 520)

[152] Utque tuo motae proles Semeleia thyrso
Ismariae celebrant repetita triennia bacchae
Byblida non aliter latos ululasse per agros…

[153] See Данов, 1965, 128ff.

classical times. The Greek colony of Maroneia, however, began to flourish soon after it was planted by the Chians. The wines of the Kikones were famous in the *Odyssey*(IX, 39-66) and the vines of Ismaros produced not less distinguished fruit. As for the god himself, apart from his obvious connection with wine and with the trieteric maenadism of the Bistonian and Kikonian women (and Orpheus), his presence is attested by the apparently ambivalent and curiously omnipresent (in our source material on the Kikones) Maron. This Maron in the *Odyssey* was a priest of Apollo.[154] We also hear that he had a *hero shrine* near Maroneia by the stream called *Odysseion*. Homer tells us that Maron was the son of Euanthes. But Dionysos is himself Euanthes. Elsewhere Euanthes is the son of Dionysos. And Euripides in the Kyklops calls Maron the son of Bacchios. We do not know the epithet of the Apollo who had his cult seat at Ismaros; but the Apollo of the not greatly distant Tenedos was called Smintheus. It is indeed curious that this very epithet which we are wont to associate exclusively with Apollo is what links him elsewhere with Dionysos.

We look first to the literary antecedents of the Augustans; Still there is nothing in what we do actually have to account for this literary-geographical shift, which seems at times to amount to nothing less than a *Sehnsucht nach Norden*, for the unsullied snows of Thracian Haemos or Rhodope and for the untrammeled passions of the Thracian Bassarai. Was it as direct descendants of the *Urmaenads* that they were singled out? Shall we then assume a new flurry of maenadic activity in Thrace, intenser, more dramatic?

There is an answer, if only a partial one: history and empire, and Augustan myth and propaganda which were intended to celebrate and explain both. And perhaps ironically the Thraco-Phrygians origins, which were conceived in myth as history, were truer than the makers of myth would have cared to own. Recent history had brought many Romans to the foothills of Pindos, Pangaion and Rhodope. And *social engineering* had made citizens of Rome permanent and unwilling residents of the Thracian outposts of empire. It was in the plains of Rhodope that the Republic had died; poetic convention after Vergil understandably makes Thessalian Pharsalos and Thracian Philippi one place. It was here, Horace tells us, that his courage cracked. Memories of Pompeius evoked memories of Philippi and thoughts of Edonian maenads. Not since Anakreon's day had Thracian maenads been so well served by the poets: the typical had once again become the topical.

---

[154] See Гочева, 2008, 259-266.

CHAPTER III

BACCHEIA. GREEK DIONYSIAC FESTNESS

The *trieterides hemerai* we know from a Suda gloss (Basil., 2) continued to be celebrated quite late in the Greek East, notably in Bithynia and Pergamum. Such was the force of tradition that well into the Christian era this seemingly unnatural, albeit intriguing, biennial festival rhythm still imposed itself upon the otherwise mostly annual pattern of mens' lives which the annual calendars of their contrivance merely reflected with ever improved accuracy. It is impossible here to speculate about the ultimate origin of this biennial custom. Perhaps we shall never know. But we can throw some light on the problem, and speak of *intermediate* causes, or, perhaps more accurately, of *coincidences*. For in all probability the trieteric festival of Dionysos was in the early historical period roughly co-terminous with *embolimos meis,* which Herodotos speaks of as being intercalated biennially (*dia tritou eteos embolimon*).

The 3ʳᵈ century A.D. grammarian Censorinus (18, 2) probably following Varro, attests both the historical connection of the trieteric intercalation with the biennial rites of Dionysos Bacchos and the applicability of the term trieteris, which was often used to designate these rites, to the intercalated month.[155] There was thus a wealth of specific trieteric activity to be individuated and defined as *trieteric: thusiai, agones, choreumata or orchesis*, etc. as indeed the festival protagonists themselves could be defined as *trieteric*. Most often, however, as we shall see comprehensive terms were used: *trieteris* – ides, trieterica vel sim. or the comprehensive hendiadys *trieterides kai baccheusin*; or the partially comprehensive rubric, *baccheia* (*baccheumata, baccheusin*, etc.) subsumed under the more comprehensive *trieteris* or *trieterides*. This is in fact a more accurate scheme; for technically speaking not all trieteric festival activity was *baccheia* or *baccheusin,* though obviously this term itself covers such a range of activity and mood, that the entire festival could without much difficulty be described as *bacchic*; indeed the *public* festival was interfused with bacchic elements and personages from start to finish. For those members of the community, who had taken part earlier in the *month* in the *restricted* or segregated phases, which were properly called *baccheia*, were formally and ceremonially *re-integrated* into the whole community in the feast of *pasa polis*,

---

[155] Itaque annos civiles sic statuerunt (sc. Veteres in Graecia civitates), ut intercalando facerent alternos duodecim mensum, alternos tredecim, utrumque annum separatum vertentem, iunctos ambo annum magnum vocantes. Idque tempus trieterida adpellabant, quod tertio quoque anno intercalabatur, quamvis bienni circuitus et reversa dieteris esset; unde mysteria, quae Libero Patri alternis fiunt annis, trieterica a poetis dicuntur.

which as we shall see in the next chapter bore the specific name, *Katagogia*, in the Ionian cities and at Athens. This was the culminating phase of the *Trieterides* of Dionysos Bacchos.

Finally, we must consider a terminological point of the utmost significance: by far the most common trieteric designator is the term *baccheia* and its cognates simply undefined with respect to its periodicity; for baccheia was a biennial phenomenon. There is in fact a great deal of evidence beginning in the classical period and extending for well over half a millennium which explicitly attests the combination of *trieterides* and *baccheia*. On the other hand, there is not once piece of evidence, which attests an annual periodicity. From this point on, therefore, the term *baccheia*, etc., when used, will be understood to connote bienniality as the Greeks themselves certainly will have understood it. The *First Homeric Hymn* is probably our earliest direct evidence for the universal celebration by the Greeks of the *Trieterides* of Dionysos Bacchos. In this case, however, the poet has chosen to speak of *men* (*anthropoi*) and not merely of *Greeks*.[156] Whether we are entitled to conclude that the poet's intention was quite so universalizing as say, the god's own account of the diffusion of his cult in the opening lines of the *Bacchae* we cannot know for certain. But no matter, for if there were not *barbaroi* included in this rubric,we can confidently assume that the reference is to the Greeks and not just some Greeks. Thus it's known that the Greek city-states more or less universally held biennial festivals in honour of Dionysos and that these festivals were everywhere "traditional" almost certainly already in the Archaic age. But from Herodotos we can deduce a certain mid 7th century *terminus ante quem* for *trieterides* and *baccheia* in Ionian Miletos. And Milesian *trieterides* and *baccheia* in the Archaic age enable us in turn to deduce a sub-Mycenaean *terminus ante quem* for mainland practice, i.e. prior to the "Ionian settlement". Herodotos (4. 108), however, once again attests the universal celebration of the *Trieterides* in the Greek world contemporary with himself as does the *parodos* of Euripides'*Bacchae*. And Diodoros (4. 3) attests the continuity of these trieteric celebrations through the Hellenistic age for Greece in general although he singles out the Boeotians and Thracians for special mention. Diodoros goes on to speak specifically about the biennial *baccheia* of women, which we normally designate by the term *maenadism*, and it is amply clear that this *baccheia* is meant to be subsumed under the broader rubric of the *Trieterides*. In this same passage he seems to allude to another feast of the trieteric festival, namely, the *Katagogia*,

---

[156] Kai hoi anastēsousin agalmata poll' eni nēois.
   Hōs de ta men tria, soi pantōs trietērisin aiei
   Anthropoid rezousi telēessas ekatombas.

casting his reference and the specific verbal reminiscence *katagagein ton thriambon* into the myth-historical mode.

In addition to the grand trieteric processionals which we deduce from the aetiology itself – the *triumph* and the *booty* – Diodoros refers explicitly to the *trieteric sacrifices* (*tas trietēridas thysias*). This expression is happily confirmed in an important Hellenistic inscription from Delphi which thus attests continuity at Thebes of the *Trieterides*; the specifically Theban maenadism which we easily deduce from Diodoros,[157] belongs, then, to these Trieterides. The public festival at Thebes bore the name *Agrionia* and the *public* sacrifices were made to Dionysos Kadmeios. These are one category of *thusiai*; it's known, again from Diodoros 4.3, that there was another category of *thusiai* performed in honour of Dionysos Bacchos by restricted groups of women, presumably within the familiar Dionysiac units of organization called *thiasoi*. From Plutarch and Clement and from the *parodos* of the *Bacchae* we know that groups of men, called *bacchoi*, also performed sacrifices of a kind. Thus we have at least three categories of *thusiai*; but these we can in turn divide into two basic types: telestic, i.e. initiatory sacrifices and non-telestic sacrifices. We recall that one of the first questions posed by the Pentheus to his laconic tutor concerns these Bacchic (or telestic) sacrifices. This type of anachronism points to contemporary and familiar cult practice. We cannot within the context of the present work be exhaustive in our Dionysiac diairesis; for we want to elucidate the major contours of the festival and the basic categories of ritual activity. But there is another kind of division we should make here which is important and germane not only to the question of sacrifice but to the structure of the rites as a whole. Both Plato (Phaed. 338,40) and Euripides (Bacch. 135-169), in the *Bacchae*, speak of *teletai* and *katharmoi* in connexion with *baccheia*. These *teletai* we know comprised substantial programmes of animal sacrifice; but what of the *katharmoi* which we usually render by the word *purifications*? These too, it would seem involved further slaughter (*fonoi*) and libations of blood: *They vainly purify themselves of blood-guilt by defiling themselves with blood, as though one who had stepped into mud were to wash with mud.* Herakleitos, not surprisingly, was contemptuous of ritual *katharsis*; but he leaves us with very little doubt that these Bacchic *katharmoi* entailed copious blood-letting. We in turn can now make sense of the phrase (*to panthyton etos*). On certain prescribed years there was a significant increase in the numbers of animals ritually slaughtered: the altars were redder with their blood; the air was thicker with pungent aromatics and strident strains of flutes devised to drown out the smell and sound of their death. Then, still more blood was shed in *penance* for this

---

[157] …para pollais tōn Hellenōn poleōn dia triōn ctōn bakheia te gynaikōn athroizestai…
(Diod., 4.3)

blood and pain. There can be very little doubt that these prescribed years were the trieteric years which were ushered in by the biennial feasts of Dionysos Bacchos.[158] And as far back as we can trace these festivals we have seen that they were complex: the *thusiai* of the public festival, of which both Diodoros and the Delphic inscription speak, are found also in what is probably our earliest witness – *the First Homeric Hymn*. *Maenadism* which was known to Homer and to the author of the *Hymn to Demeter*, and the so-called *trieterides thusiai* both belong to the Archaic age and to the same biennial festival. But if the *baccheia gunaikon* was but one component of this festival complex it was the one which caught the imagination of the poets for reasons that are not difficult to understand. And this quite simply is the reason why we hear more about it. The *thusiai* and the procession of images, which is also implied in the *First Homeric Hymn*, we hear very little about from pagan sources. Christian sources on the other hand care little about *maenads* real or fictive, but are veritably obsessed by the *eidola* and *eikones* of the orgiastic cult of Dionysos. It is often stated categorically by modern scholars that the Athenians of Euripides' day had no biennial winter rite. But this observation not only ignores the testimony of the *First Homeric Hymn*, Herodotos, Euripides' *Bacchae* and Diodoros, all of which indicate that the *Trieterides* of Dionysos Bacchos were held universally by the Greeks, thus making an anomalous exception of Athens; but it also ignores the explicit testimony of Plato[159] which indicates that the Athenians did indeed hold trieteric festivals and which, furthermore, suggests that this periodicity was in fact so commonplace. The reasons for this confusion are not far to seek: once again the almost exclusive focus on the aspect of the *Trieterides*, viz. *maenadism*, has obscured its festival context virtually to the point of invisibility. Admittedly in this case there is an additional *maenadic* complication – the *theoria* of Athenian women called Thyiads and their joint *oreibasia* at Delphi with the local Thiads. But there are analogues of this biennial maenadic practice elsewhere in Greece and in Thrace. It is therefore unreasonable to suppose that this maenadic *theoria* of Athenian women is a *political* attenuation or the like of once vigorous and *heart-felt* maenadism. Rather, it was one possible ritual combination, which as we have suggested above, probably has something to do with kinship organization and ritual quotas. Also, at Athens we must take into account the growing *secular* importance of the dramatic

---

[158] ...Soi pantōs trietērisin aiei

Anthropoid rezousi teleessas ekatombas

[159] ...kai hosai en heortais hamillai horōn anankaiai gignesthai, tahthenōn tois theois te kai tois meta theōn mēnōn kai hemerōn kai eniautōn kosmēthēsontai tote eite trietērides eite aukai dia pemptōn etōn eith' hopēi kai hopōs ennoian didōntōn tōn theōn taxeōs peri dianemēthosi.

festivals in general, although for us the relevant festival is the Lenaia. Indeed, the very fact that we know the Lenaia were held every year does seem to present a major obstacle. But in addition to the testimony of Plato, which is certainly relevant to this question, there is the fact that the scholia present us with conflicting accounts of the location of this particular festival. And it is this information in turn which may provide a solution. For at least some phases of the trieteric festivals of Dionysos Bacchos were held *in the mountains* (*en oressi*) or *in the fields* (*en argois*); in any case they were held *outside the city* (*pro poleos*). But there is a complication which obstructs our direct approach to this issue, namely, the question of mixed and segregated rites.

There is inscriptional evidence from the Imperial age which attests for a remote region of Greece the traditional *eis oros* for men (here called *boukoloi*) as well as for *maenads*. We may plausibly assume that these groups of votaries will have performed certain activities separately before coming together for other joint activities. There is, however, no need to conclude that this *joint* activity was an historical development in a society which was becoming increasingly more *open*, i.e., that *the separation of the sexes which was de rigeur in ritual maenadism had been given up, presumably in the interests of social emancipation.* Indeed, this conclusion is only possible if one fails to take into account the complexity of the trieteric-orgiastic festival which included as an integral part of its *original* structure at least one *mixed feast. Ritual maenadism,* i.e., the restricted performance of women *in the mountains* was, we know, still viable a short distance away from Physkos at Delphi during the same period. But already in the 5th century B.C. at Delphi men performed certain activities jointly with maenads in a thiasos. Again the *parodos* of the *Bacchae* speaks in general terms of the ritual activity of men *in the mountains* as well as of *bacchai.* Teresias and Kadmos too were got up as bacchoi, and they speak of *dancing* and going off *to the mountains* (190 ff.). In brief what the *Bacchae* (passim) attests is both the mixed ritual performance of men and women and the segregated ritual performance of women (viz. *maenadism*). Plutarch's Hellenistic source for his *Life of Alexander* attests the mixed rites of Macedonian men and women for the century after Euripides. And we have considered in passing above art historical evidence from the Roman age, which derives from Hellenistic models, which attests just much mixed festival performance. These manifestly ritual scenes showing women and men in their attenuated ritual attire reflect the same set of rites, if with a slightly different focus, as the *pretty* branch – the mixed Bacchic *type scene* more familiar to us in the poets but also common on the vases from the Archaic age on; in both mediums the ritual setting is perspicuous.[160] At the end of the *Bacchae* the maddened mother of the god's

---

[160] (Horac., 2, 19).

victim leads a *komos* back from the mountains to the town. We are told explicitly at 1143 that Agaue had left the maenads in their dances *in the mountains*. Is this a reflection of ritual? And, if so, who were the members of this *komos*? A copy of a fourth century *inscriptio* from Magnesia on Maeander may supply the answers: It quotes a Delphic oracle which instructs the Magnesians to build a temple for Dionysos and to fetch three maenads from Thebes.[161] A postscript records that this transaction was accomplished, and that the three maenads organized three *thiasoi*. A maenad named Thettale organized (*synēgagen*) the *thiasos tōn kataibatōn*. A. Henrichs, points out that the gender of the noun *katabatai* precludes it from being genuinely maenadic, i.e., restricted to women alone. He concludes that:

> *Thettale will have been the officially appointed Chairwoman of a Bacchic thiasos of men and, presumably, women, who celebrated non-maenadic revels.*

Henrichs cites another Hellenistic parallel, but one which reaches us through a Roman haze of prejudice and ignorance; Livy's account, however, preserves for us a number of interesting and important details about the periodicity of the rites in addition to alerting us to this very pattern of female leadership of men and women during some phase of the rites.

A notice from the late poet Sidonius (whose source, however, may be fairly early) attests this same pattern in the orgiastic ritual of the Thracians; it is worth quoting the passage in its entirety because of the importance of this issue: Sidonius gives us a rather elaborate simile which correlates two different activities which are obviously related in time and significance. The line which introduces the paralell is: *When, having just laid down your arms, you take them up again.*

We shall consider below another passage from Sidonius (Carm., V)[162] which attests the separate ritual performance of *Bassarai* and Thracian *mystai* at the *Trieterides*. Here, scarcely is the *oreibasia* over, and a *Bassaris* once again whirls the *thyrsos*, and stirs the *mystai* to the drums. A parade is about to

---

[161] See Henrics 1978, 121-160.

[162] Bistonides veluti Ciconum cum forte pruinas
    Ogygiis complent thiasis seu Strymonis arvis
    seu se per Rhodopen seu qua nimbosus in aequor
    volvit Hyperboreis in cotibus Hismaris Hebrum
    dat somno vaga turba simul lassata quiescunt
    orgia et ad biforem reboat nec tibia flatum.
    Vix requies iam fronde ligans rotat enthea thyrsum
    Bassaris et maculis Erythraeae nebridos horrens
    excitat Odrysios ad marcida tympana mystas. (Carm., V)

begin, and it sounds very much as though this Bassaris will lead it. This group of votaries would be called in the technical discourse of Dionysiac cult a *komos* or a *thiasos*. In Euripides' *Bacchae* it is a *komos* that Agaue leads, in the Magnesian inscription from the next century Thettale is in charge of a *thiasos*.[163] And in the Bacchic activities ascribed to Alexander on his campaigns in the East we hear of the "leading role" played by the courtesan Thais in the *epinikios komos* at Persepolis (Diod. Sicil. XVII.72).

The combined ritual performance of god's male and female Bacchic votaries with female leadership during a specific phase of the biennial festival is thus attested for Thrace as well as Greece at least as early as the 4th century B.C. But we reasonably deduce from the Theban origin of the three Magnesian *thiasoi* that this form of thiasic organization was to be found at Thebes. We may therefore assume a 4th century *terminus ante quem* for such a *mixed thiasos* at Thebes whatever its name. And it is just this mixed *thiasos* of *those who come down* from the mountains which may well be reflected in the great Dionysiac play of the previous century: the *exodos* suggests a union *in the mountains* between one of the maenads and another group of revelers and the joint descent of this *komos* from the mountains to the town. *Trieterides*, we will remember, are attested on the stones for Hellenistic Thebes, and biennial maenadism at Thebes belonged to this context; the *epinikios komos* or the *thiasos Kataibaton* (or whatever we choose to call it) also will have belonged to this context. The joint biennial rituals of men and women in the Hellenistic and later periods did not evolve out of the *more exclusive* women's orgia. These were different phases of the same festival: they were in the fifth century B.C., and almost certainly well before then.

Before we consider the case for change of location of the Lenaia at Athens on the alternate years, i.e. for the Lenaia *pro poleos* on the *on year* at Athens, we might briefly review some of the evidence for this bacchic *eis agrous* vel sim. in other non-Ionian Greek cities. From Herodotos(Hist., I, 150) we hear of a festival of Dionysos at Smyrna held *outside the city walls* (*en agrois*) in the mid-sixth century. In the same place from a much later source we hear of men *in the mountains* in connection with local *baccheia*. At Pergamum in the Hellenistic age we hear of *mysteria pro poleos*; at Mantineia in Roman times *orgia* were performed about a mile outside the city and at Elis, again about a mile from the city the Feast of the Thyia was held which was almost certainly orgiastic. Other parallels could be adduced; but those cited are sufficient to indicate the pattern which, according to Statius, at Thebes was god-taught: *Tyriis colonis / insomnem ludo certatim educere noctem / suaserat. Effusi passim per tecta, per agros…* (Stat., Tebaid II).

---

[163] See Henrichs, 1978, 82, 121-160.

Of the two traditions which appear in the *scholia* and lexicographers regarding the location of the *Lenaion*, the best represented is the one that points to the market-place at Athens. But the scholiast on Aristophanes *Archarnians* (202 and 504) and Stephanos of Byzantium, who claims the venerable authority of Apollodoros(1.150), refer to a place outside the city walls (*exō teiheos*). This discrepancy in the traditions is most plausibly accounted for on the hypothesis that Athens too like the rest of the Greek world in the Archaic and Classical periods (and probably down into Roman times) held the *trieterides* and *baccheia* (Hdt. 4.108) which in the eyes of the 5th century historian was a certain *semeion* of Greekness. We have seen sufficient evidence to infer what was probably the universal pattern, namely, that certain phase(s) of the *trieterides* were held somewhere outside the city walls whether *in the mountains* or *in the fields*; we may deduce that it is the very alternating pattern of trieteric and non-trieteric years with special events and a special *mise en scene* on the *on-year* which accounts for the discrepancies in the traditions. For there can be no doubt that *Lenaion* was the month of the *Bacchic orgia* in Ionian Asia Minor, and therefore by inference, also at Athens.

Plato attests the trieteric periodicity for certain Athenian fests although he does not name them: and the *bacchic* metaphor riddles his philosophical works, and the works of the 5th century tragedians. The sober discussions of Aristotle on the nature of bacchic *kinesis* and the otherwise inexplicable bacchic anachronism which pervades the choruses and the dialogue of the *Bacchae* are often enough quoted and discussed. But all this has failed to convince us of the reality of bacchic ritual activity in classical Athens. There seems little reason then to invoke the testimony of the late and very Christian Clement (Stromat.IV,19). But he does do one thing which the others fail to do, at least directly: he provides the critical onomastic link between the *bacchicai teletai* and the Lenaion fest. And this passage we can in turn link with an important passage in Plato's *Laws* (815c) to which we shall return at some length below. In addition we can corroborate the Lenaion-bacchic connection Clement makes with a variety of evidence including inscriptions which attests this same combination in an Ionian context. Finally, armed with this much evidence, we can enlist the testimony of the greatest of the comic poets. In the *Frogs*, which we know was produced at the Lenaion festival of 405 B.C., Aristophanes speaks quite explicitly about *bacchic rites*; and he connects with these *baccheia* – as Clement was to do – *Lenaizontes poietai*, specifically in this case his predecessor, Kratinos.[164] A few lines below Aristophanes again makes the critical connection of comedy and Dionysiac *teletai* (368). What is this *baccheia* of which

---

[164] Mēde Kratinou tou taurofagou
glōttēs bakhei etelesthe(357)

Aristophanes speaks, what are these *teletai* of Dionysos if not the *baccheia* and the *teletai* of Dionysos Baccheios, of which Herodotos, in the same century, speaks? These rites as we have seen, and we may now state categorically, were biennial. And bienniality was a fest rhythm by no means foreign to Athens.

Herodotos, our earliest witness to attest the combination of *baccheia* and *trieterides* explicitly, provides unimpeachable evidence for the universal practice of these rites among his contemporary Hellenes: the mixed population of the distant city of Gelonos held the trieteric revels, he says, because they were originally Greek.[165] The veracity of this claim is not at issue here, nor is the *origin* of the Geloni, however interesting the question it raises. The notice is important for us because it verifies the claim made in the prologue and in the *parodos* of the *Bacchae* of the historian's contemporary, Euripides, that the trieteric-bacchic rites were celebrated throughout Greece. From Herodotos (4.108 and 4.79), which attest specifically the Bacchic initiation of men in the Mileasian colony of Olbia on the Black Sea, we have plausibly deduced the same pattern of worship for Archaic Miletos. Indeed the trieteric pattern of Bacchic initiation which we deduce for Olbia from Herodotos (4.108) is confirmed for the metropolis in an Hellenistic inscription: as the inscription itself is a contract for the sale of a priesthood of Dionysos Bacchios, and the office is that of priestess, the particulars quite naturally pertain to female *baccheia*.[166] There is reference to sacrificing and initiation in the city itself and in the countryside as well as in the Milesian islands (i.e. Leros, Lepsia and Patmos) at the *trieteris*. The inscription also mentions the specific feast of the *Katagogia*, and links it not merely, by juxtaposition, with the *trieteris*, but the bacchic sacerdotal hierarchies who belongs to it, also link it with *baccheia*. Another Hellenistic inscription[167], the tomb epigram of the *leader* of the Milesian Bacchai, shows perspicuously the *private* and the *public* roles of important *bacchic* personages: chiefest among the *public* roles will have been their participation in grand trieteric processional and summing up, the *Katagogia*. Thus for the city of Miletos we can reconstruct with very little difficulty the major contours of a complex of male and female bacchic worship which we know was trieteric and for which we easily deduce an early terminus ante quem. But when we link this

---

[165] kai tō Dionysō trietēridas anagousi kai bakheuousi. Eisi gar hoi Gelōnoi to arhaion Hellenes.

[166] LSAM 48 = Jaccottet no. 150. The most detailed and important discussions of the text are those of Henrichs, from aspects of whose interpretation I differ: see Henrichs (1978) 149-152, based largely on the more detailed discussion in Henrichs (1969) 235-238.

[167] Peek, 1955) no. 1344 = Jaccottet no. 149; text also at Henrichs (1978) 148, whose translation I adapt. For discussion see Henrichs (1978) 148-149, based largely on Henrichs (1969) 225-234.

festival with the month of Lenaion, as we are entitled to do in an Ionian context, we easily obtain a sub-Mycenaean terminus ante quem. It is moreover a reasonable deduction that this same complex of worship was to be found in Bronze Age Pylos – the city of the Neleid kings from whom the founders of most of the Ionian cities claimed decent.

Bacchic initiation of both men and women, then, is attested directly and indirectly by Herodotos, while the trieteric periodicity is confirmed by Hellenistic inscriptions from Miletos, Rhodes and Kallatis[168]. Bacchic initiation of men and women is likewise attested by Euripides throughout the *Bacchae* and elsewhere in the *Bacchae* the evidence is in different forms: direct statement as in the *parodos*, myth-historical statement in the prologue and throughout the play and, not least, it is in the form of anachronism. This anachronism is evidence which supplements Herodotos (4.79), for male bacchic initiation in the 5th century if not prior to it. There is no other explanation: *ho bacchos* is not the *exarchos*; he is the lowest undifferentiated type of male bacchic votary – but nonetheless, as Pentheus sees him, a dangerous proselytizer. Herakleitos, like Pentheus, had contempt for the breed. But Dionysos the god was no mere *bacchos*: he was the son of Zeus as well as son of Semele.

In addition to the several inscriptions from the Hellenistic period which explicitly attest the biennial periodicity of bacchic initiations, there are a number either from a later period where continuity can be demonstrated at least from the Hellenistic age or from places where Trieterides are otherwise attested, which refer simply to *mysteria* or to *telein* or use the language of initiation, e.g. *neobacchos*. The Dorian states are especially well represented: Kos, Rhodes, Kallatis. And once again the very early settlement of the so-called Dorian Hexapoleis gives us early *terminus ante quem* (as does the foundation date of Megarian Herakleia which in turn founded Kallatis) for biennial Bacchic initiations among the Dorian states of the Greek mainland. *Trieterides* and *mysteria* are attested separately in two different sources for Ptolemaic Egypt but it seems most reasonable to connect these two notices thus bringing both *mysteria* and *trieteric* dramatic *agones* within the larger festival context. Here it is perhaps of interest that the month of the *Trieterides* at Ptolemais was Peritios – the Macedonian month of January. Peritios was also the intercalated month at Alexandria. And we happen to know that the Dionysiac procession of Ptolemy Philadelphos was held in the middle of the winter. It is very tempting, therefore, to look upon this *pompe* a the Macedonian equivalent of the Attic-Ionian feast of the *Katagogia*. But perhaps this most interesting notice we have, which attests both the biennial periodicity of Bacchic initiation and the complexity of these rites in some detail, including the *mixed feast*, reaches us through the

---

[168] See Henrichs 1978, op. cit.

distorting lens of Roman historiography. Livy's account is muddled, but not beyond comprehension. Not apprehending the complexity of the trieteric-orgiastic rites, the multiple phases, segregation and mixis, etc. the Roman historian has arranged his evidence in a developmental pattern; things naturally go from bad to worse: originally segregated rites become *mixed*; annual rites become monthly and the number of days increases. It is not even clear that the historian understood the significance of the term *biennium* in his source material, i.e. the biennial pattern of initiation of which *biennio* (39.10.16) and *biennio proximo* (39.13.14) are almost certain reflections. Indeed the modern translators of Livy have not understood this term. The sequence of dates Livy gives at the end of his account of the Roman suppression of Bacchic activity in Southern Italy, namely, 186 B.C. 184 and 182, seems to confirm the entirely expected fact that Trieterides and *baccheia* were indeed held in Magna Graecia during the Hellenistic period. Sophokles after all had represented *Italy* as a headquarters of Dionysiac religion already in the Classical period. This same pattern of initiation and other "bacchic" activity is perspicuous once again in one of our major bacchic cult inscriptions from the Imperial age. And we can use this inscription to illustrate one very important point which will throw some light upon the perplexing and apparently contradictory annual and even monthly rhythms Livy must have found in his source. We have stated categorically that *baccheia, bacchica, baccheuein*, etc. was properly a biennial activity, i.e., that it belonged to the biennial complex of worship known in antiquity by the generic term *Trieteris* or *Trieterides*. On the other hand, the congregations of *bacchoi* (Baccheia) who controlled the initiations and other *private* trieteric events, naturally observed other Dionysiac feasts, some of which were manifestly unconnected with the trieteric-orgiastic form of Dionysiac worship. But there was yet another category of ritual activity which was relevant to bacchic congregations, namely, feasts which were correlated with the trieteric celebrations.

We can be virtually certain of one of these, namely, the *amphieterides*, and certain too, that it was the most important in this category. To translate this difficult word as *yearly* or *year by year* as LSJ do, is to fail to apprehend the fact that this is a relational term meaning *both years* or *each of two years* the years of binary pairs and not years in a linear series of single years. *Both years* then, are effectively the *on year* and the *off year* in a series composed of two year units, i.e., the trieteric year and the non-trieteric year; in terms of Dionysiac ritual these are the years of extensive sacrificial slaughter, of baccheia and, not least, of divine epiphany and the year of no *baccheia*, of sacrificial restraint, if not in fact, abstinence, and of non-epiphany; and in terms of Dionysiac myth these are the year of plenty and the year of fruitlessness, famine and infertility.

But as it is the manner of myth to turn the regular and repeated *formulae* of ritual into *historical hapax genomena* we naturally lose the alternating rhythm of plenty and want almost entirely – that is, we lose the repetition of these alternations. It is quite reasonable to suppose that in time the term *amphieteris* came to designate the non-trieteric year alone. Thus the *amphieteris*, which is mentioned in the Dionysiac inscription from Pltolemais in Egypt and manifestly correlated with the trieteris of the same inscription, would be technically the feast held on the *off year* and the *on year* but effectively, the feast held on the *off year* only; for the trieteric celebrations will have understandably eclipsed the amphieteric celebration of the *on year*. The Iobacchoi of Athens celebrated *amphiterides* as well as the (by definition) biennial *baccheia*; we plausibly assume a correlation between these two sets of feasts; but whether we are right to speak of the monthly meetings of the Iobacchoi, which were held on the 9th day, as also correlated or connected specifically with the biennial *raison d'etre* of these bacchoi, it is impossible to say. Obviously they will have been to a certain extent; but in any case the parallel with Livy's account is perspicuous, and its relevance, self-evident. It seems, therefore, to make some sense to speak of the festival of the Lenaia as being amphieteric, i.e., of being celebrated on both the trieteric and non-trieteric year, and in case of the former as being attached to or connected with a series of special trieteric events including copious sacrificing, *baccheia*, epiphany, etc. and celebrated in a special place. The same would of course apply elsewhere, e.g. at the Boeotian feast of the Agrionia. In fact once we have established the categories the evidence seems to make more sense: the non-bacchic Lenaia in Classical Athens was not an attenuation of once wild rites but the *off year* festival and the *lenaizontes poietai* whom Clement connects with a *bacchic rite* are not the fantasy creatures of a mendacious protesting Christian but one set of the ritual performers of the alternate *bacchic year*. Finally as we have seen above the Lenaion-bacchic connection is attested for Asia Minor as early as Herakleitos and as late as the so-called Orphic Hymns.[169] The Orphic Hymn to Amphietes makes clear a number of things: the *on-year* and *off-year* correlation, the epiphany and non-epiphany which belongs to each respectively and finally the bacchic identity of the god in whose honour these paired festivals were held (Hymn. Orph. 53). Here, the *amphieteris* is effectively the mid-point in the two year period between divine epiphanies – between the *Trieterides* – when the god slept his holy two-year Bacchic sleep in the halls of Persephone. Then no sweet persuation, no reminders of the joys of the trieteric song and dance or of the *komos*, which, as Trieterikos, he led in his own person[170] no bounty of fruits can raise him; then, he is

---

[169] See West, 1983.
[170] Autos kōmon egeirēi

(*hthonion*); then, as Herakleitos said, *Dionysos and Hades are the same*- this is the same god in whose honour, on the other year, they held the mad Lenaion feast at which he himself participated. Firmicus Maternus is a late and un-friendly witness; but he gives us some valuable information about male *bac-cheia* at the Trieterides; the Cretans he says:

> *festos funebres dies statuunt et annum sacrum trieterica consecration componunt, omnia per ordinem facientes, quae puer (sc. Dionysus) mo-riens aut fecit aut passus est...*[171]

This passage is interesting and important here for two reasons. First, it gives us the explicit link we need to connect the *private baccheia* of the bacchoi, namely, the indoor, *sacred meal*, with the Trieterides – a connection we should have deduced in any case. Those aspects of male bacchic activity, which were carried on very much in the open, we shall return to below in another connec-tion. Otherwise, the trieteric periodicity is explicitly attested for this species of *Baccheia* only at Rhodes, although we necessarily deduce it from an Hellenistic inscription for the *bacchoi* of Kallatis whose *sacred meal* is attested on a late inscription.[172] And Plutarch, in his comparison of certain feasts of the Jews with the *baccheia* of the Greeks, attests this type of feast for Greek bacchoi universally in his own age. It seems indeed virtually certain that the reference to the specifically Athenian *trieterike panteleia*, which begins Plutarch's discus-sion, and at which certain things were (*rēta kai didakta tois myoumenois*) which we cannot be told, is just such a reference to the indoor activities of the *bacchoi*. Some of these *omnia per ordinem facta* of which Firmicus speaks, then, are the same *poioumena* of the indoor *baccheia*. The second point of in-terest concerns how the Greeks perceived their own Bacchic feasts. Indeed here too we see that they understood their own ritual activity as commemora-tive performance celebrating, in this case, the death of the god by ritually re-enacting every detail of that event in the proper order – both the actions of the god and the actions of his *murderers* (*omnia... quae puer aut fecit aut pas-sus est facientes*). The *crime* of the Titans is thus the sacramental *blessing* of the biennial *baccheia* of the *bacchoi*. The complementarity of ritual pollution and grace become the polarities of the myth and the doctrine of cult: of crime and of beatitude. The *bacchoi*, then, segregated and behind closed doors *commem-orated* the *death* of the god, as the *bacchai* in their segregated open air perfor-mance *commemorated* the activities of their *mythical* counterparts – the

---

[171] De err. 6.

[172] The mythical Titans are stationed in the *inner part* of the palace where the crime was to be commeted; then we hear of the construction of a temple-tomb which is reminiscent of the tomb of Dion. in the temple of Apollo at Delphi.

maenads of old – the maddened ministers of a rejected and vengeful god.[173] The *mixed fe*ast of satyrs and bacchai, pans and paters, was likewise understood as being commemorative; and in this case the periodicity of ritual has made its way into the mythical *aition*. [174]The *sacred meal* of the *bacchoi* and the *crime* of the Titans belong *myth-ritually* together. And Titan myth was used in male *baccheia*. [175] Similarly, the Pentheus myth belongs to female *baccheia*. Finally, the myth of the victorious "return" of the god and his unruly crew belongs to yet another phase of the trieteric festival of Dionysos Bacchos – its final one, namely, the *Katagogia*. The communis opinio holds that the *Katagogia* was an annual spring event commemorating the arrival or *return* of the god by sea. The majority of scholars connect it with the Attic feast of the Anthesteria, in spite of the fact that this is probably the best attested of the Attic festivals with respect to the activities of its individual days and there is no explicit or implied connexion to be found in any of our source material.

There are three major, interrelated, points which speak against this assumption. First, periodicity: the assumption of an annual rhythm – a reasonable enough a priori assumption when dealing with most religious festivals – is entirely ex silentio, and at the very least, questionable in the case of this particular god. In fact, this is the one feast of the Trieterides which has its biennial periodicity *explained* explicitly in its mythological aetiology: the *India campaign* (*ek tēs Indikēs*) of the god Dionysos is the specific aetiology of the trieteric *Katagogia* – the Feast of the Victorious Return.[176] The second point relates to the name of the feast itself as evidence for the periodicity. In addition to the rather obvious verbal allusions to the feast name in Diodoros' discussion of the Trieterides (*thriambon d' auton onomasthēnai fasin apo tou prōton… katagagein…thriambon…*), there is the fact that *Katagogia*, which is usually rendered in this context as the *Feast of the Return*, quite transparently refers to an epiphany of the god. Now the only epiphany of the god Dionysos, which is explicitly attested (and it is attested universally and over many centuries), is the trieteric epiphany. Where epiphany is otherwise attested, but periodicity is not made explicit in our source material, it can usually be deduced, e.g., for the

---

[173] …tas de gynaikas…thysiazein tō theō kai bakheuein kai katholou tēn parousian hymnein tō Dionysou. mimoumenas tas historoumenas to palaion paredreuein tō theō mainadas…

[174] …ek tēs Indikēs… tēn eis Thēbas epanodon poiēsasthai. Trietous de diagegenēmenou tou sympantos hronou fasi tous Hellēnas apo tautēs tēs aitias…

[175] Teitanōn prolegein mystais…

[176] …eis Thebas epanodon poiēsasthai. Trietous de diagegenēmenou, tou sympantos hronou, fasi tous Hellēnas apo tautēs tēs aitias agein tas triēteridas, mytholoousi d' auton kai lafyrōn ēthroikota plēthos. Katagegein de protōn tōn hapantōn thriambon eis tēn patrida.

feast of the Thyia at Elis; here, the nature and the location of the feast, the plurality of priests, and not least, its very name, all provide strong presumptive evidence for its bienniality. In fact to a Greek the name, *Katagogia*, itself, would connote bienniality, just as the term baccheia did. Furthermore, it is quite inconceivable that a feast celebrating by its very name, the *return* of the god, could have been held on the *off-year* in the same month as his trieteric epiphany, e.g. at Ephesos, in January.

Finally, the inscriptional evidence we do have from the Hellenistic and the Imperial age relating to the *Katagogia* shows quite plainly that the feast was temporally juxtaposed to events called *baccheia*; the Hellenistic inscriptions from Miletos and Priene, moreover, indicate not only that the *Katagogia* was composed of bacchic elements, but that these elements dominated the *public* processions. Yet another Hellenistic inscription from Miletos attests both the *private* and *public* roles, namely, in *baccheia* and *pompai*, of the leader of the Mileasian bacchants. [177] The same inscription shows that the implements and concrete effects of the *baccheia*, which are here called *orgia*, were prominent in the otherfeast:

Alkmeonis led the Milesian *bacchai* to the mountains and carried "all the sacred implements of the orgia" (*orgia panta kai hira*) before the entire population of the city. The doublet, introduced by kai... kai, thus connects both "private" and "public" functions of this head bacche, and indicates their mutual significance in the concrete term, orgia, which were common to both ritual episodes. Indeed, the Milesian cult ordinance of 276/5 attests just such a role for the priestess of Dionysos Bacchios in the *Katagogia*.

The last point we should note has been mentioned before; it is simply that this plurality of priests and priestesses of Dionysos Bacchios is otherwise attested only for the biennial baccheia or mysteria, although, as we have seen above in connexion with the late bacchic association at Athens, they will have celebrated other Dionysiac feasts along with the rest of the population. But it is Dionysos Bacchios himself with whom the case must rest: the inscriptions from Miletos and Priene leave us with no doubt that it is this god who is celebrated at the *Katagogia* by the entire population of the city, whereas earlier in the trieteric festival he had been celebrated by restricted groups of the population (*bacchoi and bacchai*). These same groups had invoked the god at their respective feasts, and he had in some sense made his presence felt. But it was at the culminating feast of the *Trieterides* that he came *autos*. A *victorious* campaigner home from foreign wars. Ritual commemorated myth-history; this is how the Greeks explained it. These elaborate *pompai* were biennial because the India campaign *had lasted two years*. And it was at these biennial feasts that the

---

[177] See Henrichs, 1978,121-160.

Greeks thought the god made his epiphany among men (Diod. 4., 3). Nilsson himself has no doubts about the epiphany of the god at the feast of the *Katagogia*:

> … *dass die Priester und Priesterinnen des Dionysos Bakchios an den Katagogien den Dionysos herbeiführen sollen; es gab also eine Epiphanie.*[178]

An epiphany of Dionysos Bacchios must have been trieteric. For these reasons then, it seems virtually certain that the *Katagogia* were trieteric and closely connected in time and significance with the Bacchic initiations.

Our principal witnesses are few in number, but they span half a millennium. Both the earliest, Herakleitos, and the last, the anonymous Christian author of the *Acta Timothei*, attest the feast of the *Katagogia* specifically for the Ionian city of Ephesos. Plato, our third witness, speaks of *baccheia* and *Katagogia* in his native city without mentioning the specific festival name. To complete this picture we must turn to an elaborate "bacchic" conceit of the kind Plato frequently employed on more modest scale. From Herakleitos we learn that there were *mysteria*, which will certainly have included the Dionysiac, at Ephesos which were considered *traditional* already in the 6th C B.C[179].

They were a part of the "state religion" at Ephesos, and by plausible inference, in the other Ionian cities as well during the Archaic age which is in fact what we have already deduced from Herodotos (4, 79, 108). *Teletai* and *mysteria*, sometimes synonymous terms, sometimes complementary, and the grand bacchic summing up, the *Katagogia*, which will have included a variety of rites, but most conspicuously, the mixed and motely parade, were all part of the Lenaion *Trieterides* which were celebrated in honour of Dionysos Bacchos. Herakleitos, like Plato, seems to have condemned the lot; but in the following notice he is quite plainly referring to the culminating Bacchic parade.

Plato's testimony is admittedly more difficult of access in this case than either Herakleitos or the *Acta* because it contains no reference to either the festival name or to the date it was held. But quite apart from the specific festival participants he does name, who mark the events as trieteric-orgiastic, there is his explicit statement connecting the events he describes with baccheia. Fortunately for us, Plato is a highly reliable source who is here in a mood of absolute earnestness. [180]

---

[178] See Nilsson 1985.

[179] Ta vomizomena kat' anthropous mystēria anierosti myeuntai. (Her. B 14 b)

[180] Hosē men bakheia t' estin kai tōn tautais hepomenon, has Nymfas te kai Panas kai Selenous kai Satyrous eponomazontes hōs fasin, mimountai katōnōmenous, peri katharmous te kai teletas tinas apote lountōn, sympan touto tēs orhēseōs to genōs… (Laws, 815 C)

There are two points of which we must be aware if we are not going to misread this evidence: first, the satyrs, seilen uses, pans and nymphs, who participate in this festival, are masquerading humans got up, as they themselves saw it, as their mythical counterparts who belonged to that *original* comos of the victorious, returning, god – a mythological construct to which the ritual performances of their distant ritual predecessors had given rise. The second point is merely a corollary of the first, namely, that the satyrs were in no degree less *real* than their trieteric festival counterparts, the *bacchai* (maenads – or sometimes, as here, called nymphs). It remains merely to note the obvious: that the *aidoia* in our Herakleitos fragment should be understood as being attached to the reveling men. In the following notice the masks and *unseemly attachments* belong to the same class of men. These mortal ministers of the god were called by various names; but throughout antiquity they were normally called satyrs.

Our last notice is in some ways our most important one in spite of its lateness. For it provides us with two certain pegs: Most important, is of course the feast name itself, which in an Ionian context must belong to Dionysos and to no other god. This supposition is confirmed by the individual elements – the masks, the *proschemata aprene*, the *purgatio animae*, and, not least by its January date; but our source not only informs of the month, he also gives us the exact date and duration of the feast. This is in some ways our fullest account of the culminating feast of the Lenaion *Trieterides*. It will be useful therefore to begin, as it were, at the wrong end of the historical time scale using the rubrics the Christian source supplies supporting and supplementing this evidence with the testimony of Herakleitos and Plato as well as other sources, pagan and Christian:

Masks and *Unseemly attachments*: Herakleitos we recall had spoken of a *hymn to the shameful parts*. It was these *unseemly attachments* themselves and the various things that were done with them – *attached* and "unattached" – which in large part will have constitutes the activity designated by the term *paidia: tous de Satyrous tois prosgelota synergousin epitēdeumasin hrōmenous...* Clement, who quotes these lines of Herakleitos (fr. 15), goes on to remark that all these goings on were *not so much for the sake of bodily intoxication as for the shameful display of licentiousness.* The *phalloi* were after all as Clement (Protr. 2.30) well knew fake. But the mock character of the ritual did not lead to lighter sentences of guilt in Christian authors. This *holy display of the unholy*, which both Herakleitos and the Christian Clement lament as shameless and obscene will of course remind us at once of countless amusing scones of Attic Black and Red Figure Vases of men with masks (usually partly *melted*) and *unseemly attachments* fore and aft. [181] It is noteworthy that by Hellenistic times the masks

---

[181] See Carpenter, 1993, 185-206.

of the satyrs have *melted* almost entirely in Dionysiac ritual scenes, and have become, as it were, *bacchic symbols* in Dionysiac iconography. They lead a static existence devoid of ant animating agent. As such they lie propped up against other Dionysiac *symbols* – the pillar, the liknon, etc. or they are held objectively in the hands of ritual participants. Different ages pick their different symbols. There are a variety of explanations: we have considered above the changes in artistic focus in the representation of Dionysiac *phalloi*. What we must beware of in the extreme are conclusions about fundamental changes of innovations in ritual based upon observed changes in "symbolic representation".

Song and Dance: We can be more or less certain that the songs mentioned in our earliest witness will have been accompanied by certain rhythmical movements of the body, i.e., by dancing. The same thing applies to the songs of the *Acta*. In fact, in the century after Herakleitos, we have testimony which explicitly connects satyrs with the dances of the *Trieterides*.[182] The progress of satyrs and the other *daimones* at this festival is variously described. Some authors refer to their *pompe* or *pompeuein*.[183] Others refer to them as a marching "choros" – or simply as a "choros". Plato (Laws 815C) could sum up the entire activity by referring to it as a type or category of dance. At Pergamum also we hear of trieteric dancing – in this case of boukoloi; but we know that satyrs, called in this case silenoi, participated in the Pergamene rites together with these boukoloi. Finally, Lucian attests the participation of both satyrs and boukoloi and others in a notice on *bacchike orchesis* which he defines as *satyric*.[184]

Ataxia and Mixis: Our Christian source speaks of the disorderly incursions made by one group of festival participants upon other. Dionysiac "disorder" results in a mingling of classes – of slave with freeman, of male with female, of sacred with the apparently profane. The appearance is indeed chaotic, and the crossing of the demarcating lines of sex, social class, etc. seems dangerous and reprehensible. In spite of the confusion of this account, however, we see at a glance that the elements are the familiar ones: the women, here called *semnai* are in all probability the city's official bacchai, who would be from a good class. The pranks and piracy are known from a variety of sources.[185] The good-natured Dionysiac aggression at Ephesos had its parallel elsewhere in

---

[182] Eur. Ba. 130-134 cf. Plat. Laws, 835A

[183] On the ritual *mimesis* cf. Plat. Laws 815C; Diod. 4.3; Of course Herakl. fr. 15 is the earliest evidence for the pompai; on the *victory spoils* of which Diod. speaks cf. Plut. Mor. 527D and Himer.Or. XIV 26. Cf. also Athen. 5. 197E; ib. 198A and 199B.

[184] I. Perg. 485; SIG, 1115; On the well-bred participants, cf. St. August. Epist. 17.4.and n. 32. On *orchesis* see Plat. Laws 815C.

[185] It is tempting to connect this with what may be a reflection of ritual at Ba. 748-64 – the raid on the Theban villages.

Greece; certainly it has its parallels in other cultures. Historical *imitations* are always of interest for they often follow their models most scrupulously. Alexander on his return from the East is said to have *imitated* Dionysiac *baccheia* and *komos*; this is characterized as a *mixed* group of male and female with much music, bacchic sport and disorder.[186] Again, in Philostratos' description of the *wine miracle* at Andros, which we know from independent sources was celebrated on the nones of January and was biennial, the same idea recurs. Even at this third remove from *reality* the use of the word Lenai for the more common bacchai, maenads or nymphs, may well reflect the mid-winter date of the *real* feast.[187] Certainly the most interesting notice we have on this aspect of this festival is again from a Christian source.[188] In this case, however, the word *ataktos* not only provides, as it were, the recurrent theme of the passage, but the festival is even called by that name, i.e., *The Festival of Disorder*. There cannot be a great deal of doubt that the events described here – even allowing for Christian *exaggeration* – represent some part of the festival which we know as the *Katagogia*. For it took place on the island of Patmos which was one of the three Mileasian islands. The Hellenistic inscription from Miletos, which is our earliest source for the actual name of the feast, attests the trieteric Bacchic initiations (in this case of women) for the Milesian islands as well as for the city itself and surrounding country-side. Again, the plurality of priests points to the trieteric-orgiastic form of Dionysiac religion. Most of the details in this Christian account are in fact not only credible but they are attested in unbiased pagan sources: the *pollution* of the house of the god, the wine and Dionysiac dining, the plurality of priests and, from Dionysiac myth, even the binding of the hero and the collapse of the antagonist's house. Here, however, the hero and victor is not the god, but the enemy of the god. The antagonists of theomachy have changed: *theos* and *ho monon ontos Theos*. The scales are unbalanced. The Christians too could learn to skillfully employ Dionysiac myth to the advantage of their god. The *ataktos polymixia* presents a number of obvious difficulties. For we have long since been taught to divest the term orgia of most of its old and unsavory connotations. We cannot within the confines of the present work devote the necessary attention to this difficult problem; but we can note in passing that it is perhaps time for a reappraisal. Certain Thracian and Skyth tribes and clans practiced this type of *ataktos polymixia*. The Greek themselves, pagan once that is, were certainly discreet about their orgia – all of them. But there are occasional fleeting references to bacchic *mixis* and there

---

[186] Plut. Alex. 67; cf. Arr. An. 6.28! cf. also Plat. Laws, 672Bf.
[187] Plei de kai Dionysos epi kōmon tēs Androu…Satyrous de anamix kai Lēnas agei kai Seilēnous…ton Gelōta te …kai kōmon Philostr. Im. I 25; see Paus. 6.26.2.
[188] Acta Joannis, 127f.

are faint adumbrations of incest in this connexion. There are still other hints and signs – if we are looking for them – in the scholia and lexicographera.[189] If in fact our Christian source is right in broad outline in his account, then we should gravely err, were we to conclude that this bacchic *genetic pooling* was postprandial pranks and play alone.

Images: The author of the *Acta* speaks of *eidololatreia*. Christian attacks on *idolatry* were particularly vigorous, as the emotional appeal in the *Acta* shows: ō, andres *Ephesioi me eidolomaneite*. Once again, however, we find that the early Greek philosophers anticipated them by over half a millennium. Herakleitos was indeed terse and contemptuous where the Christians, especially Clement who quotes him often, were prolix and passionate. But it is these very Christian attacks which draw our attention to the *eidola* and *eikones* of the pagan Greeks. To the latter these were simply too omnipresent and too familiar to merit much attention, at least in such a direct fashion. To the Christians they were unnecessary, unwanted and odious as were the bloody sacrifices made to them or associated with them. These practices were not restricted to Dionysiac trieteric-orgiastic feasts; our earliest notice on the *Trieterides* attests as it happens both the trieteric *hekatombs* and processions of images destined to be set up in the temples and shrines (on alternate years) – by implication.[190] Clement spoke about the myth-historical *Pentheus* who *reveled through a frenzy of idols*(*bakheuōn eidolois*). He has given a ritual interpretation to two very puzzling lines from the *Bacchae* thus giving indirect testimony of the use of images (and perhaps of mirrors)[191] in bacchic ritual. Elsewhere he had spoken of the *theologia tōn eidolen*, i.e., about a *logos* – an explanation – of the images of the gods. If this is orgiastic Dionysiac ritual he is here speaking of – a plausible, if not a certain inference, then who were this plurality of gods, who were concretely represented (*eidola or prosopa*)? The host of deities represented in the corpus of *Orphic Hymns* is a late starting point: those who were individually addressed were *participants* at the Dionysiac *trieterides in the persons* of their *prosopa* – their *images*. Dionysos himself was *present* at his biennial feasts *in the flesh (autos)*. This is admittedly at this stage simply speculation which we cannot pursue at any greater length here. But it might be instructive to recall in conclusion that it was exactly the amphieteric Dionysos – the *off-year Bacchos* who was invoked to come to the feast. According to this hypothesis, theoppo-

---

[189] See schol. ad Ar. Plut. 975

[190] On the sacrificing of raw meat to the image of Dion. see A. Henrichs, 1969, 233f. The policy of promotion of paganism in Bithynia in the face of the growing threat from Christians would of course be in large measure the promotion of Dionysiac religion. Filling the temples with sacrificial victims was one proof of proper pagan credentials, see Plin, Epist. X 96.10.

[191] Cf. e.g. Harpokr. ; see also Clem. Al. Strom. IV, 121.

sition of the *emphanes daimon* – the one god who was *seen* and *unseen* and a plurality of gods who were merely and sempiternally *eikones eidolon* will have been built into Dionysiac trieteric-orgiastic ritual.

Purification: These rites were kathartic, and included slaughter of animals (*phonoi*) and libations of blood (*plēthos haimatōn ekheontes*). We recall that Herakleitos had referred contemptuously to those who "purify themselves of blood guilt through blood". And Plato (*Laws* 815C) has called these rites of masquerading satyrs, silenoi, nymphs, etc. *katharmoi*. The same term, together with *teletai*, is found in the *parodos* of the *Bacchae*. Finally, Varro confirms the expression in the Acta about the festival participants acting as though they were doing something *psychopheles*.[192] This "mystic purpose", which even our Christian source acknowledges, is indeed difficult at first glance to reconcile with the other overtly playful and even obscene features of the feast. But Plato confirms the purificatory purpose of these rites of satyrs and pans and nymphs not only in the *Laws* but also in the *Republic* the reference to Orpheus and his books and the emphasis on *thusiai* as well as on *hedonai* and *paidia* point the direction of the bacchic. And it is in that very context that the philosopher speaks of *teletai* and *katharmoi*.[193] We must recall here that it was Dionysos who Plato called the god of *telestike* (Rep. 364E).[194] The bacchic cult in fourth century Athens was by no means ritually defunct nor was it doctrinally flaccid. Once we have acknowledged the universal practice of the trieteric-orgiastic rites and the continuity of this practice in most parts of the Greek world from the Archaic age (and probably earlier) at least through the Hellenistic period, then we expand the amount and increase the number of categories of our evidence. For it then becomes not only unnecessary, but in fact meaningless, to introduce into the religious picture of fourth century Athens groups of men or a set of rites both called "Orphic" as people distinct from Bacchoi or as ritual distinct form or additional to the *bacchikai teletai* and *katharmoi*. The *teletai* of *Laws* (815C) and *Faedo* (69C) were certainly bacchic; and the *katharmoi* of *Laws 815C* were certainly bacchic. There is then no reason why we cannot be equally certain about the *teletai* and *katharmoi* at *Republic* 364E. For our evidence for the trieteric festival as a whole points to a multiplicity of phases, a complexity of rhythms, a diversity of functions and a great variety of moods. *Teletai, thusiai, paidia, hedonai, katharmoi*, all belonged to the trieteric festival

---

[192] Mystica autem Iacchi ideo ait, quod Liberi patris sacra ad purgationem animae pertinebant, et sic homines eius mysteriis purgabantur, sicut vannis frumenta purgantur... Liber pater, in cuius mysteriis vannus est, quia, ut diximus, animas purgat... (Serv. I 165).

[193] See Фол, 2002, 85ff.

[194] See Dodds, 1951, 64ff.

of Dionysos Bacchos. This multiplicity, this complexity, this diversity of mood and purpose, belonged to the rites of this and to those of no other Greek god. Certainly, this complex was not the creation of an *Orpheus* or of succeeding generations of recusant and schismatic priests called *Orphikoi* or called by any other name. But they were not effective *reformers* of the rituals of that cult; indeed, we have no right to hypothesize new and different rituals introduced by doctrinal *purists* who came forth from the *pauperum tabernis* to threaten the rich and unclean with all the races of the damned and with the deep, dark squalor of their kingdom. To posit a new or a schismatic cult is to fail utterly to apprehend the inherent complexity of Dionysiac religion and to understand the significance of its apparent ritual oppositions and the consequent complex variety of its doctrine. In addition, there were different ways of focusing on the rituals and the doctrines of this cult: it offered *release* from present toil and pain and pleasure in the present moment; and it offered *release* from a metaphysical pollution which was *recapitulated* in the individual of the species, with a view to a blessed existence in a tribalistic, *otherworldly* future. This religion was far too variegated and complex to be comprehended by the viewing lens of any one individual at one time: Euripides' was a broad sympathetic focus; but it is partial. Plato's was no less broad; but it was unsympathetic. The poet and the philosopher were looking for different reasons at different aspects of the same cult. Herakleitos in his terse enigmatic fashion comprehended these two aspects – *to para podon kalon* and *ta ekei kala* – in a line: Those who *went down* as the *clansmen* of Dionysos Bacchos to the world below, were not a different class of men from those who *reveled in the mountains*. Only in the *Bacchae* the stress, which is *tragic* one, is on the *makarismos* in the here and now.[195] Both authors are speaking of those who have been *initiated* into the rites of Dionysos Bacchos. Dionysiac religion was indeed catholic in its appeal, its rituals were profound in their consequences. It seems that for a time in what was perhaps its "finest hour" at the end of the Archaic age it had an important ritual-doctrinal centre: Magna Graecia was, as it were, the ecclesiastical *Rome* of the period, and the *religion* of this *holy see* was the religion of Dionysos Bacchos. In the eyes of Sophokles it was still a head-quarters of the Dionysiac church in the fifth century B.C. Herodotos seems to have thought of it as the most important centre of Dionysiac *learning*. For reaching through the mists of *Orpheus* legend to the concrete and the credible he installed the well-known

---

[195] Maker hostis eudaimōn
    teletas theōn eidōs
    biotan hagisteuei kai
    en oresi bakheuōn
    hosiois katharmoisin…(72-77)

sage from Kroton in the *chair* of Dionysiac *wisdom*. Arignote after all, by some accounts Pythagoras' daughter, by others his pupil, had written a *Bacchica* and the *teletai Dionysou*.

Thus we have the three major categories of Dionysiac myth, each one reflecting one of the three major phases of the Trieterides. We have by now expanded our conception of the trieteric-orgiastic festival of Dionysos with respect to both the extent of its contours and the complexity of its component feasts and phases. It remains to consider briefly this same complex in a somewhat different light: we will try to apprehend some of the basic rhythms of trieteric ritual. These rhythms have the shape of binary oppositions but they are ritual complementaries. Here too is a source of confusion: if these basic patterns are not understood, erroneous conclusions are easily drawn about development and change where there was essentially constancy and continuity; false oppositions are posited from a complex that is basically one and unified and historical variation is deduced from the variety of integral ritual.

We may begin our discussion with a specifically Thracian notice; for we have seen enough evidence at this stage to feel reasonably certain that the trieteric-orgiastic form of Dionysiac worship in Thrace was not greatly different from the Greek rites. [196] The author of the following lines, Sidonius, is very late indeed, but his source may well have been an early one. It is clear that Sidonius is speaking of the *separate* ritual performance of *bacchai* and of *bacchoi*. The scene he sketches, in however brief a compass, reminds us in part of the picture of Bacchic worship suggested by the group of hymns to Dionysos belonging to the corpus traditionally called *Orphic*. The majority of these hymns prescribe a variety of aromatics for burning – *thumiamata aromata*. [197] And they speak of *thiasoi* and of *komoi* and of the god's leadership of the latter. As early as Homer the god was a *maddened* guest at his own feast. Here the god sends the *mystai* whirling to the altars; this is bacchic performance, i.e., restricted, which is nevertheless conducted very much in the open. In Herodotos'account of the Bacchic initiation of the Skythian Skyles the spying Skyths were able to observe the *god-possessed* king as he went by *reveling* in the *thiasos*(4.79).

Herodotos would know the Bacchic details and the language from his Greek contemporaries, who, he leads up to believe, held these rites pretty much everywhere. What went on behind closed *bacchic* doors we are not told, nor would the Skyths have been able to see. We know from numerous sources

---

[196] Non Bacchum trieterica exserentem
    describam et tremulas furor efesto
    ire in Bassaridas vel in fulatos
    aram ad turi cremam rotarc mystas. (Carm., V)
[197] See, Йорданова, 2013, 123-134.

some of the most obvious signs of the Bacchic *madness* which seized the initiates: the wry-neck pose, the corporeal rotations to the noise of the drums, the dissonant cries and drones. Plutarch, by far our most prolific source, also tells us that there was obscene language at the shrines. There were sets of days, when there were meals of *raw flesh* and rendings and in turn there were other days of fasting and universal lamentation and again cursing at the shrines.[198] He concludes his rather unlovely, prosaic, account quite fittingly with a quotation from a dithyrhamb by the Boeotian poet Pindar. In the poem the local Dionysiac scenario has been transferred to the heavenly halls of the immortals: the kettle-drums, the castanets, the yellow torches, the loud groans of women and the neck-throwing mob of men and their frenzied shouts. Pindar has given a sketch of the part of the *cosmic liturgy*; and this heavenly liturgy is a mirror image (with divine protagonists) of the rites of mortal men on earth; there were Underworld analogues.

The idea of the Heavenly liturgy was an integral part of Orthodox Christianity, and was often represented in the painting of the Eastern Church. Its root too, or the roots of the conception, are in all probability Dionysiac as this passage of Pindar and the *parodos* of the *Bacchae* seem to show. Pindar begins his account with one of the traditional formulas of beautitude; although the text is fragmentary here, enough remains to discern the essential features(Pind. II, Ol., 70, b). The immortals are imagined as performing a bacchic rite; and the mortal men who know the manner of this rite are called *blessed* – here - wise. This doctrine sounds like Dionysiac *theology*: a logos was expounded to the initiates about the gods – about their *ritual* roles and about their relationships. Clement can throw some light here; for he speaks of Orpheus the Thracian who after the *exposition of the orgia* and the *account about the images of the gods brings in a recantation consisting of truth*. here it is *the logos* about the gods and about their rites we must consider; and since we know that the trieteric rites of Dionysos were indeed thick with images, it seems in principle probable that there is an intrinsic connexion between the *theologia of the images* and the *teletai* of the gods of which both Pindar and Euripides speak half a millennium before Clement.

Perhaps it would be well to consider the *makarismos* passage of the *parodos* of the *Bacchae* (72-77) because both the Greek and the usual English renderings are in some degree ambiguous. Dodds has translated these lines:

> *O blessed is he who, by happy favour knowing the sacraments of the gods, leads the life of holy service....*

---

[198] Hēmerai apofrades kai skythropai en hais ōmofagiai kai diaspasmoi nēsteiai te kai kopetoi pollaxou palin te aishrologiai pros hierois…(Alex. 6-7).

To render (*teletas theōn eidōs*) *knowing the sacraments of the gods* is simply to preserve in English the ambiguity of the Greek. The problem then is really the nature of the genitive: is it in effect an *objective* genitive or is it a subjective genitive? Obviously the traditional interpretation, and it seems an unquestioned one, is that it is indeed a kind of objective genitive: *rites in honour of the gods*. In this case then the participal phrase (*teletas theōn eidōs*) is the broadest rubric in lines 71-82 and the ensuing list of participles and finite verbs jar both logically and grammatically. If, however, we take the genitive as subjective, and translate *knowing the gods (own) rites*, then the symmetry of the Greek is preserved as are the two basic categories of the *makarismos*: *logoi* and *praxis*. The chiasmus, then, consists of two participles flanking the two finite verbs which, as it were, summarize bacchic experience. But if there is still doubt about this reading of the Greek, the Pindar dithyramb must remove it: there is no ambiguity whatsoever here in the Greek.[199] It seems virtually certain, therefore, that Euripides too is referring to a *heavenly liturgy*.

Pindar's account, then, as a *mirror image* of terrestrial ritual, is no less valid as *evidence* for Dionysiac cult practice than the drabbest prose account. As stated above our information on the formal acts of Dionysiac purification is rather scanty. These, however, ritual symmetry demands, and we do know for a fact that there was *fasting*. The question is, therefore, how will the fast have been ceremonially portrayed. In the Bacchae the *state of grace* induced by the *eating raw* is symbolized by the description of the Dionysiac miracles which follows immediately upon that of the Dionysiac *hunt* and omophagy.[200] These are the traditional features of the *locus amoenus*; but they belong specifically to a sub-category of it, namely, the *Golden age*. Milk, wine, honey and the smoke of incense belong conceptually to a *state of innocence*, to an imagined time before the knives of the killer-priests were poised at the necks of beasts who brayed fearfully amidst the pious benedictions of their slaughterers. In ritual terms, they belonged to a period of atonement. Thus the *thumiamata aromata* on the smoking altars and in the pungent braziers are not merely sacrifice, they are the formalized converse of ritual slaughter – acts of ritual purification.

It is a doctrine which turns the ritual pollution into a kind of metaphysical *hapax genomenon*. Only Euripides (Ba. 138f.) concentrates on the homeopathic *cure*, and turns the ritual pollution itself – *omophagia* – into a form of grace – *charis*. The taking of animal life is one of the major components – *cross-culturally* – in the concept of the *Fall*. Empedokles is again of particular

---

[199] Hoian Bromiou teletan… Ouranidai histanti…(Pind., Fr. 70b,6).
[200] Rei de galakti pedon, rci oinō, rci de melissan nectari
Syrias d' hōs libanou kapnon ho Bakheus anehōn (Eur. Bach. 142 - 145)

interest,[201] although this is perhaps not the best example because of the special problem connected with the apparently cyclical nature of the cosmic dispensations. Plato (Rep. 364) is rife with problems we cannot deal with at the necessary length in the present work; here it must suffice to note that the *lyseis* and *katharmoi* are effected *dia thusion.*

The castanets or rattlers are often shown on the monuments or referred to in literary sources.[202] They are proscribed in the inscription relating to the *sacred meal* of an association of *bacchoi* from Smyrna.[203] It is perhaps in this context, then, that we should consider the troublesome lines from the Hippolytos (952-954). We need not reject the traditional interpretation of the phrase (*pollōn grammatōn kapnous*); but it might not be amiss to see here an additional *Orphic* reference, namely, to the altars smoking with frankincense and myrrh instead of with the blood and fat of roasting flesh, both of which were integral parts of bacchic ritual. To this same ritual and this same cult belonged an accumulation of *logoi* of diverse kinds: *myth, theologia, doctrinal sophia.* Of these *logoi* much from the last two categories, by the time of Euripides, had long since been associated with the name of Orpheus. The supposed, ritual-doctrinal contradiction between the *Orphic* and the *bacchic* is a scholarly construct: *Orphic* purity could not be achieved except through ritual pollution. It was the myth of cult which treated of that *pollution*, at least for the most part, and it was the doctrine of the same cult which treated of the resultant *purity.* That cult was bacchic and in the eyes of most of the Greeks its *baccheios anax* par excellence was the Thracian *sophos aner* Orpheus. We, then, rightly construe the verb *baccheuein* in the preceding passage from the Hippolytos as a *vox propia* and not a metaphorical usage. Plutarch, we will recall, had given us an outline of this ritual pattern: there were a set of *unpleasant days* during which both rendings of animals and raw feasts and fastings and lamentations took place. The fact that Plutarch begins and ends with the Dionysiac, seems indeed to preclude the inference that the *nesteiai* and the *kopetoi* belong to other gods and other cults. The god too, like his votaries, feasted on *raw flesh.* What exactly this portion of raw flesh will have been we cannot guess. But there is no indication that this was a particularly savage affair; and there is absolutely no reason to assume that this ritual was mitigated over the centuries. In modern Thracian *Dionysiac* ritual we are told of a *kreanomia* of *raw*

---

[201] See e.g. fr. 466, 1.9f.,

[202] Cf. e.g. Pind. Dithyrh. 2 = n. 91 above; cf. Ar. Nub. 260 and schol.ad loc.

[203] Nilsson's interpretation of this line is most peculiar; see DM 138. He not only misses the point of the prescription: "The mystae had to use other instruments of a similar kind". Indeed the proscription implies the use, certainly the existence, of castanets, in another phase of the ritual activities. It is the class of noise-makers that is relevant and not the species.

meat before the *feast*. Indeed this Thracian rite looks a rather tidy affair. It is in fact the combination of Dionysiac *sparagmos* and *omophagia* which gives us the particularly savage picture of the rites we are wont to hold at least as the Ur-type. It is possible that *sparagmos* in its ritual context was also a less savage affair than what is suggested by the word itself or than that represented on numerous vases. But there is no escape from the fact that the procurement of the animal skins for ritual attire – particularly that of the fawn – will have been an unpleasant procedure. The separation of the skin from the flesh and bone will have entailed a certain amount of pulling and rending. And it does seem that the skin of the fawn, the *nebris*, was a *sine qua non* of bacchic initiation. It is, then, very difficult indeed to get away from the proposition that the god's bacchic votaries did in fact feast on raw flesh. The *parodos* of the *Bacchae* must refer to human, and not divine, consumption of raw meat. Euripides and Plutarch were good pagans with Dionysiac sympathies; indeed Plutarch had been initiated into the Dionysiac *mysteries* as he himself tells us. Intelligent Christian proselytisers, like Clement, attest the same practice in colourful, but not exaggerated terms. They knew better. Firmicus Maternus on the other hand attests the same practice, but indulges in the kind of exaggeration (*vivum laniant dentibus taurum*), that enables habitual sceptics to dismiss his testimony. Clement twice speaks of the omophagy of male votaries of Dionysos Bacchos.[204] Feasting *raw* and fasting, ritual enactment of a pollution and the attainment, through pollution, of the state of bacchic *grace*, runnels of blood and runnels of milk, the stench of slaughter and the sweet-smelling smoke of incense, *violent* acts and pious words – all these are the complementary oppositions of the integral complex of bacchic ritual.

Certainly one of the most important questions we can ask about bacchic initiation is that of *cui bono*. Here, however, it is not possible to do more than indicate the direction the enquiry should take. What class of people stood to benefit by initiation? And what, in concrete terms, was the nature of that *bonum*? In the first place we are severely hampered by the sheer dearth of information about the individuals who were initiated in the earlier periods. We are, however, not entirely at a loss. The earliest individual we know of by name, and in this case, even class, to have been initiated into the rites of Dionysos Baccheios was the Skythian Skyles. We also know that Skyles was something of a *half-breed*. Herodotos' account is once again open to the charge of *bacchic ornament* which is normally but a prelude to outright dismissal; for it is always easier to dismiss than to defend apparently embroidered accounts. But for our purposes here, it is quite irrelevant whether this tale is embroidered; or even if the entire account is apocryphal, its significance for us remains unaltered. For

---

[204] (Shol. In Protr. 2.3; 119.1)

such accounts tend to conform in certain ways even slavishly, to the exact pattern of the thing being claimed – in this case a Bacchic initiation. In other words, the basic categories in the story will reflect real ritual categories, e.g., *initiation* itself (*Dionysō Baheiō telesthenai*); divine possession and *madness* (*ho theos lambanei*) and (*mainesthai*); the *reveling* in the technical sense (*bakheuonta*); those special bacchic *tiasos* within which the initiates *reveled* (*pareiē syn thiasō…min bakheuonta…*).Now it stands to reason also that the individual seeking bacchic membership, in the story, would belong to one of those categories of individuals in "real life" who traditionally sought it. In fact we happen to know the name of another individual in the century after Herodotos who was initiated, as our late source puts it, into the *Orphica*. It was Antisthenes the orator. He too was a kind of *half-breed*: he was not a *full-blood*ed Athenian. Half-breeds, then, and *agennetai* (*men without fathers*) will in all probability have comprised the majority of those seeking initiation into the rites of Dionysos Baccheios at least in the earlier periods. The members of the clans did not need the services of this god. This *time* belonged by birth to those who could trace their descent from the gods; and if its significance had waned in the world above by Classical times, in the world below it was retained. This assurance given by Sokrates to one now preoccupied with his prospects in that world, concludes a very lengthy description of an Underworld *locus amoenus* where the initiated perform the holy rites *sub specie aeternitatis* as did Pindar's Ouranidai in their own celestial halls.

The *initiated* have become the clansmen of Dionysos and Herakles. We have considered above how the concepts of *adoption* and of *adopted clan* may well in this case be more than mere analogy or metaphor. The social structure of the Underworld and the limitations it imposes on certain classes of individuals as well as the benefits it confers upon others are a mirror image of *ta enthade*. But while the situation on earth might change with the passage of time, it was rigidly fixed below at the time of conceptualization – forever. Neither the centuries of Greek democracy nor those of Hellenistic cosmopolitanism, nor indeed the vast stretches of time that have intervened, have significantly altered man's conception of social structure of this Graeco-Christian Hell. The model was and still is a tribalistic one; for it was conceived and fixed at that *stage* of social organization.

The *olbion genos* may well have been *blessed* or *happy* – exactly because they could, in some sense at least, call themselves a *genos*. We cannot speculate at any length about the concrete *earthly* rewards of this *adoption*. But one of them was certainly the assurance of burial: the place, the act and the unction, and perhaps, the tending of the tomb.The fear of no burial was general and very great among the ancients. One way of removing this fear, then, for those who were barred from the burial plots of the clans or from those later provided by the state, was through initiation into the rites of Dionysos Bacchos, i.e., adoption into the *bacchic genos*. It is, moreover, not very difficult to conceive of a set of *Jenseitserwartung* accreting in the long reaches of tribal time round this concrete bacchic privilege. But if the changing social conditions on earth did not in any significant way alter man's basic conception of *life on the other side*, they will certainly have altered the needs of those without the proper *connections*. The less privileged classes would increasingly, if only very gradually, improve their lot and their possibilities. Conversely, in the course of time, those, who did not need the concrete earthly rewards conferred by bacchic initiation, might turn to the increasingly independent body of doctrine which had long since accreted round the rituals of the bacchic cult, and been elaborated, refined and elevated, though the *path* to *redemption* was still through ritual. The division between ritual and doctrine was of course never complete in fact; but the apparent independence of the latter in so much of our source material has led to the scholarly dichotomy of the *Orphic* and the *Bacchic* – a vision of piousness and purity on the one hand and of playfulness and pleasure, if not of outright savagery, on the other. Indeed, in time, bacchic initiation for some would become merely *trendy*: those with impeccable pedigrees would join the *church*, carefree Imperial ladies and bored gentlemen who could hold out little hope for their immortal souls in the next world, received the bacchic sacraments in pious expectation of pleasure in this.

It is remarcable that the system of divine appellatives of Thracian Dionysos is close to this of the Thracian heros, evidenced in the inscriptions. Dyonisos is the one who *bestows prosperity*, he is defined as *brining fruits, who makes the fruit grows, donor of vines* etc.[205] Along this line he is associated with Hades, and in Crestonia he is worshipped by the Byzalts as the distributor of fertility. (Ps. Arist. De mir. Ausc. 842). Precisely as a heros and in the epiphany of *noble bull* Dyonisos is summoned and expected in the early liturgical hymn of the women from Elida, quoted by Plutarch.[206] For archetypical heroic essence of the god evidence also the main structural elements of his mythological biography, where are noticeable the three stages of human life – from child to old man - with their relevant statuses[207]. In the same semantic line of Dyonisos as heros-patron is also the act of establishing the royal dynasty of Haropydes, bound by the sharing of the mysterial secret as a mark of selectiveness (Diod. III. 65. 4-7).[208]

---

[205] Дечев 1952, 43.
[206] Elthein, ērō Dionyse, Aleion es naon . (Quaest. gr. 36, 299, 538, A 4); Nilsson 541.
[207] Маразов 1992, 125.
[208] From this point of view could be interpreted also the definitions of Euripidus - *wise hunter* и *ruler, king*, hunter (Eurip., *Bacchae*, 1189-1192).

The studied sources support the conclusion that in the middle of VI c. BC in Hellas is performed a religious synthesis of ingredients from non-Greek origin that generate the divine characteristics of Dyonisus[209]. In it is noticeable the idea of the circle of the nature, supported by the believers by orgies and mysteries. Thus beneath the surface of the summary image there are noticeable elements associated with the Minoan Zagreus, with the Thracian-Frygian Sabazios and with the Mediterranean deities of the vegetation. It is possible the semantics of the Dionisos female orgies in Hellas to be associated with some earlier Thracian-Pelasgean magical rituals aiming inclusion to the life power of the Cosmos. (Heinrichs 2011, 114). Dressing in animal skins, the touch to the greenery of the ivy and yew, the prophesy during the ecstatic dances and invocation of the god, are all actions of the order of the catharsis magical practices.

---

[209] Михаилов 1972, 224; Фол 1994, 243-244; Dimitrov 2012, 26ff, (with some critical notes).

APPENDIX

TRANSLATED SOURCES

Euripides, *Bacchae* [210]

Dionysus

I, the son of Zeus, have come to this land of the Thebans—Dionysus, whom once Semele, Kadmos' daughter, bore, delivered by a lightning-bearing flame. And having taken a mortal form instead of a god's, [5] I am here at the fountains of Dirke and the water of Ismenus. And I see the tomb of my thunder-stricken mother here near the palace, and the remnants of her house, smouldering with the still living flame of Zeus' fire, the everlasting insult of Hera against my mother. [10] I praise Kadmos, who has made this place hallowed, the shrine of his daughter; and I have covered it all around with the cluster-bearing leaf of the vine. I have left the wealthy lands of the Lydians and Phrygians, the sun-parched plains of the Persians, [15] and the Bactrian walls, and have passed over the wintry land of the Medes, and blessed Arabia, and all of Asia which lies along the coast of the salt sea with its beautifully-towered cities full of Hellenes and barbarians mingled together; [20] and I have come to this Hellene city first, having already set those other lands to dance and established my mysteries there, so that I might be a deity manifest among men. In this land of Hellas, I have first excited Thebes to my cry, fitting a fawn-skin to my body and [25] taking a thyrsos in my hand, a weapon of ivy. For my mother's sisters, the ones who least should, claimed that I, Dionysus, was not the child of Zeus, but that Semele had conceived a child from a mortal father and then ascribed the sin of her bed to Zeus, [30] a trick of Kadmos', for which they boasted that Zeus killed her, because she had told a false tale about her marriage. Therefore I have goaded them from the house in frenzy, and they dwell in the mountains, out of their wits; and I have compelled them to wear the outfit of my mysteries. [35] And all the female offspring of Thebes, as many as are women, I have driven maddened from the house, and they, mingled with the daughters of Kadmos, sit on roofless rocks beneath green pines. For this city must learn, even if it is unwilling, [40] that it is not initiated into my Bacchic rites, and that I plead the case of my mother, Semele, in appearing manifest to mortals as a divinity Now Kadmos has given his honor and power to Pentheus, his daughter's son, [45] who fights against the

---

[210] Euripides. The Tragedies of Euripides, translated by T. A. Buckley. Bacchae. London. Henry G. Bohn. 1850.

gods as far as I am concerned and drives me away from sacrifices, and in his prayers makes no mention of me, for which I will show him and all the Thebans that I was born a god. And when I have set matters here right, I will move on to another land, [50] revealing myself. But if ever the city of Thebes should in anger seek to drive the the Bacchae down from the mountains with arms, I, the general of the Maenads, will join battle with them. On which account I have changed my form to a mortal one and altered my shape into the nature of a man. [55] But, you women who have left Tmolus, the bulwark of Lydia, my sacred band, whom I have brought from among the barbarians as assistants and companions to me, take your drums, native instruments of the city of the Phrygians, the invention of mother Rhea and myself, [60] and going about this palace of Pentheus beat them, so that Kadmos' city may see. I myself will go to the folds of Kithairon, where the Bacchae are, to share in their dances. whom she bore to Zeus.

Chorus

From the land of Asia, [65] having left sacred Tmolus, I am swift to perform for Bromius my sweet labor and toil easily borne, celebrating the god Bacchus[1]. Who is in the way? Who is in the way? Who? Let him get out of the way indoors, and let everyone keep his mouth pure [2], [70] speaking propitious things. For I will celebrate Dionysus with hymns according to eternal custom.

1 Lit. shouting the ritual cry εὐοῖ.

2 E. R. Dodds takes this passage "Let everyone come outside being sure to keep his mouth pure". He does not believe that there should be a full stop after the third τίς.

Chorus

Blessed is he who, being fortunate and knowing the rites of the gods, keeps his life pure and [75] has his soul initiated into the Bacchic revels, dancing in inspired frenzy over the mountains with holy purifications, and who, revering the mysteries of great mother Kybele, [80] brandishing the thyrsos, garlanded with ivy, serves Dionysus.

Go, Bacchae, go, Bacchae, escorting the god Bromius, child of a god, [85] from the Phrygian mountains to the broad streets of Hellas—Bromius,

Chorus

Whom once, in the compulsion of birth pains, [90] the thunder of Zeus flying upon her, his mother cast from her womb, leaving life by the stroke of a thunderbolt. Immediately Zeus, Kronos' son, [95] received him in a chamber fit for birth, and having covered him in his thigh shut him up with golden clasps, hidden from Hera.

And he brought forth, when the Fates [100] had perfected him, the bull-horned god, and he crowned him with crowns of snakes, for which reason Maenads cloak their wild prey over their locks.105] O Thebes, nurse of Semele, crown yourself with ivy, flourish, flourish with the verdant yew bearing sweet fruit, and crown yourself in honor of Bacchus with branches of oak [110] or pine. Adorn your garments of spotted fawn-skin with fleeces of white sheep, and sport in holy games with insolent thyrsoi . At once all the earth will dance— [115] whoever leads the sacred band is Bromius—to the mountain, to the mountain, where the crowd of women waits, goaded away from their weaving by Dionysus. [120] O secret chamber of the Kouretes and you holy Cretan caves, parents to Zeus, where the Korybantes with triple helmet invented for me in their caves this circle, [125] covered with stretched hide; and in their excited revelry they mingled it with the sweet-voiced breath of Phrygian pipes and handed it over to mother Rhea, resounding with the sweet songs of the Bacchae; [130] nearby, raving Satyrs were fulfilling the rites of the mother goddess, and they joined it to the dances of the biennial festivals, in which Dionysus rejoices. [135] He is sweet in the mountains [1], whenever after the running dance he falls on the ground, wearing the sacred garment of fawn skin, hunting the blood of the slain goat, a raw-eaten delight, rushing to the [140] Phrygian, the Lydian mountains, and the leader of the dance is Bromius, evoe! The plain flows with milk, it flows with wine, it flows with the nectar of bees. [145] The Bacchic one, raising the flaming torch of pine on his thyrsos, like the smoke of Syrian incense, darts about, arousing the wanderers with his racing and dancing, agitating them with his shouts, [150] casting his rich locks into the air. And among the Maenad cries his voice rings deep: "Go, Bacchae, go, Bacchae, with the luxury of Tmolus that flows with gold, [155] sing of Dionysus, beneath the heavy beat of drums, celebrating in delight the god of delight with Phrygian shouts and cries, [160] when the sweet-sounding sacred pipe sounds a sacred playful tune suited [165] to the wanderers, to the mountain, to the mountain!" And the Bacchante, rejoicing like a foal with its grazing mother, rouses her swift foot in a gamboling dance.

Teiresias

[170] Who is at the gates? Call from the house Kadmos, son of Agenor, who leaving the city of Sidon built this towering city of the Thebans. Let someone go and announce that Teiresias is looking for him. He knows why I have come and [175] what agreement I, an old man, have made with him, older still: to twine the thyrsoi, to wear fawn-skins, and to crown our heads with ivy branches.

Kadmos

Dearest friend, for inside the house I heard and recognized your wise voice, the voice of a wise man; [180] I have come prepared with this equipment of the god. For we must extol him, the child of my daughter, [Dionysus, who has appeared as a god to men] as much as is in our power. Where must I dance, where set my feet [185] and shake my grey head? Show me the way, Teiresias, one old man leading another; for you are wise. And so I shall never tire night or day striking the ground with the thyrsos. Gladly I have forgotten that I am old.

Teiresias

Then you and I have the same feelings, [190] for I too feel young and will try to dance.

Kadmos

Then will we go to the mountain in a chariot?

Teiresias

But then the god would not have equal honor.

Kadmos

I, an old man, will lead you, an old man, like a pupil.

Teiresias

The god will lead us there without trouble.

Kadmos

[195] Are we the only ones in the city who will dance in Bacchus' honor?

Teiresias

Yes, for we alone think rightly, the rest wrongly.

Kadmos

The delay is long; come, take hold of my hand.

Teiresias

Here, take hold, and join your hand with mine.

Kadmos

Having been born mortal I do not scorn the gods.

Teiresias

[200] We mortals have no cleverness in the eyes of the the gods. Our ancestral traditions, and those which we have held throughout our lives, no

argument will overturn, not even if some craftiness should be discovered by the depths of our wits. Will anyone say that I do not respect old age, [205] being about to dance with my head covered in ivy? No, for the god has made no distinction as to whether it is right for men young or old to dance, but wishes to have common honors from all and to be extolled, setting no one apart.

Kadmos

[210] Since you do not see this light, Teiresias, I will be your interpreter. Pentheus, child of Echion, to whom I gave control of this land, is coming here to the house now in haste. How fluttered he is! What new matter will he tell us?

Pentheus

[215] I happened to be at a distance from this land, when I heard of strange evils throughout this city, that the women have left our homes in contrived Bacchic rites, and rush about in the shadowy mountains, honoring with dances [220] this new deity Dionysus, whoever he is. I hear that mixing-bowls stand full in the midst of their assemblies, and that they each creep off different ways into secrecy to serve the beds of men, on the pretext that they are Maenads worshipping; [225] but they consider Aphrodite before Bacchus.

As many of them as I have caught, servants keep in the public strongholds with their hands bound, and as many as are absent I will hunt from the mountains, [I mean Ino and Agave, who bore me to Echion, and [230] Autonoe, the mother of Actaeon.] And having bound them in iron fetters, I will soon stop them from this ill-working revelry. And they say that some stranger has come, a sorcerer, a conjuror from the Lydian land, [235] fragrant in hair with golden curls, having in his eyes the wine-dark graces of Aphrodite. He is with the young girls day and night, alluring them with joyful mysteries. If I catch him within this house, [240] I will stop him from making a noise with the thyrsos and shaking his hair, by cutting his head off. That one claims that Dionysus is a god, claims that he was once stitched into the thigh of Zeus—Dionysus, who was burnt up with his mother by the flame of lightning, [245] because she had falsely claimed a marriage with Zeus. Is this not worthy of a terrible death by hanging, for a stranger to insult me with these insults, whoever he is? But here is another wonder—I see Teiresias the soothsayer in dappled fawn-skins [250] and my mother's father—a great absurdity—raging about with a thyrsos. I shrink, father, from seeing your old age devoid of sense. Won't you cast away the ivy? Grandfather, will you not free your hand of the thyrsos? [255] You persuaded him to this, Teiresias. Do you wish, by introducing another new god to men, to examine birds and receive rewards for sacrifices? If your gray old age did not defend you, you would sit in chains in the midst of the Bacchae,

[260] for introducing wicked rites. For where women have the delight of the grape-cluster at a feast, I say that none of their rites is healthy any longer.

ChorusLeader

Oh, what impiety! O stranger, do you not reverence the gods and Kadmos who sowed the earth-born crop? [265] Do you, the child of Echion, bring shame to your race?

Teiresias

Whenever a wise man takes a good occasion for his speech, it is not a great task to speak well. You have a rapid tongue as though you were sensible, but there is no sense in your words. [270] A man powerful in his boldness, one capable of speaking well, becomes a bad citizen in his lack of sense. This new god, whom you ridicule, I am unable to express how great he will be throughout Hellas. For two things, young man, [275] are first among men: the goddess Demeter—she is the earth, but call her whatever name you wish; she nourishes mortals with dry food; but he who came afterwards, the offspring of Semele, discovered a match to it, the liquid drink of the grape, and introduced it [280] to mortals. It releases wretched mortals from grief, whenever they are filled with the stream of the vine, and gives them sleep, a means of forgetting their daily troubles, nor is there another cure for hardships. He who is a god is poured out in offerings to the gods, [285] so that by his means men may have good things. And do you laugh at him, because he was sewn up in Zeus' thigh? I will teach you that this is well: when Zeus snatched him out of the lighting-flame, and led the child as a god to Olympus, [290] Hera wished to banish him from the sky, but Zeus, as a god, had a counter-contrivance. Having broken a part of the air which surrounds the earth, he gave this to Hera as a pledge <protecting the real> [1]Dionysus from her hostility. But in time, [295] mortals say that he was nourished in the thigh of Zeus, changing the word, because a god he had served as a hostage for the goddess Hera, and composing the story. But this god is a prophet—for Bacchic revelry and madness have in them much prophetic skill. [300] For whenever the god enters a body in full force, he makes the frantic to foretell the future. He also possesses a share of Ares' nature. For terror sometimes flutters an army under arms and in its ranks before it even touches a spear; [305] and this too is a frenzy from Dionysus. You will see him also on the rocks of Delphi, bounding with torches through the highland of two peaks, leaping and shaking the Bacchic branch, mighty throughout Hellas. But believe me, Pentheus; [310] do not boast that sovereignty has power among men, nor, even if you think so, and your mind is diseased, believe that you are being at all wise. Receive the god into your land, pour libations to him, celebrate the Bacchic rites, and garland your head. Dionysus will not compel women [315] to be modest in regard to Aphrodite, but in nature [modesty dwells always] you must look for that. For she who is modest will not be corrupted in Bacchic revelry. Do you see? You rejoice whenever many people are at your gates, [320] and the city extols the name of Pentheus. He too, I think, delights in being honored. Kadmos, whom you mock, and I will crown our heads with ivy and dance, a gray yoke-team but still we must dance; [325] and I will not be persuaded by your words to fight against the god. For you are mad in a most grievous way, and you will not be cured by drugs, nor are you sick without them.

ChorusLeader

Old man, you do not shame Phoebus with your words, and honoring Dionysus, a great god, you are prudent.

Kadmos

[330] My child, Teiresias has advised you well. Dwell with us, not apart from the laws. For now you flit about and have thoughts without thinking. Even if, as you say, he is not a god, call him one; and tell a glorious falsehood, [335] so that Semele might seem to have borne a god, and honor might come to all our race. You see the wretched fate of Actaeon, who was torn apart in the meadows by the blood-thirsty hounds he had raised, [340] having boasted that he was superior in the hunt to Artemis. May you not suffer this. Come, let me crown your head with ivy; honor the god along with us.

Pentheus

Don't lay a hand on me! Go off and hold your revels, but don't wipe your foolishness off on me. I will seek the punishment of this [345] teacher of your folly. Let someone go quickly to the seat where he watches the flights of birds, upset and overturn it with levers, turning everything upside down; [350] and release his garlands to the winds and storms. In this way I will especially wound him. And some of you hunt throughout the city for this effeminate stranger, who introduces a new disease to women and pollutes our beds. [355] If you catch him, bring him here bound, so that he might suffer as punishment a death by stoning, having seen a bitter Bacchic revelry in Thebes.

Teiresias

O wretched man, how little you know what you are saying! You are mad now, and even before you were out of your wits. [360] Let us go, Kadmos, and entreat the god, on behalf of him, though he is savage, and on behalf of the city, to do no ill. But follow me with the ivy-clad staff, and try to support my body, and I will try to support yours; [365] it would be shameful for two old men to fall down. But let that pass, for we must serve Bacchus, the son of Zeus. Beware lest Pentheus bring trouble to your house, Kadmos; I do not speak in prophecy, but judging from the state of things; for a foolish man.

Chorus

[370] Holiness, queen of the gods, Holiness, who bear your golden wings along the earth, do you hear these words from Pentheus? Do you hear his unholy [375] insolence against Bromius, the child of Semele, the first deity of the gods at the banquets where guests wear beautiful garlands? He holds this office, to join in dances, [380] to laugh with the flute, and to bring an end to cares, whenever the delight of the grape comes at the feasts of the gods, and in ivy-bearing banquets [385] the goblet sheds sleep over meneaks foolishness.

Chorus

Misfortune is the result of unbridled mouths and lawless folly; but the life of quiet [390] and wisdom remain unshaken and hold houses together. Though they dwell far off in the heavens the gods see the deeds of mortals. [395] But cleverness is not wisdom, nor is thinking on things unfit for mortals. Life is short, and on this account the one who pursues great things does not achieve that which is present. In my opinion, [400] these are the ways of mad and ill-advised men.

Chorus

Would that I could go to Cyprus, the island of Aphrodite, where the Loves, who soothe [405] mortals' hearts, dwell, and to Paphos, fertilized without rain by the streams of a foreign river flowing with a hundred mouths. Lead me there, Bromius, Bromius, god of joy who leads the Bacchae, [410] to Pieria, beautiful seat of the Muses, the holy slope of Olympus. There are the Graces, there is Desire; there it is [415] lawful for the Bacchae to celeb **Chorus**

The god, the son of Zeus, delights in banquets, and loves Peace, giver of riches, [420] goddess who nourishes youths. To the blessed and to the less fortunate, he gives an equal pleasure from wine that banishes grief. He hates the one who does not care about this: [425] to lead a happy life by day and friendly night and to keep his wise mind and intellect away from over-curious men. [430] What the common people think and adopt, that would I accept.

Enter a servant

Servant

Pentheus, we are here, having caught this prey [435] for which you sent us, nor have we set out in vain. This beast was docile in our hands and did not withdraw in flight, but yielded not unwillingly. He did not turn pale or change the wine-dark complexion of his cheek, but laughed and allowed us to bind him and lead him away. [440] He remained still, making my work easy, and I in shame said: "Stranger, I do not lead you away willingly, but by order of Pentheus, who sent me."And the Bacchae whom you shut up, whom you carried off and bound in the chains of the public prison, [445] are set loose and gone, and are gamboling in the meadows, invoking Bromius as their god. Of their own accord, the chains were loosed from their feet and keys opened the doors without human hand. This man has come to Thebes [450] full of many wonders. You must take care of the rest.

Pentheus

Release his hands, for caught in the nets he is not so swift as to escape me. But your body is not ill-formed, stranger, for women's purposes, for which reason you have come to Thebes. [455] For your hair is long, not through wrestling, scattered over your cheeks, full of desire; and you have a white skin from careful preparation, hunting after Aphrodite by your beauty not exposed to strokes of the sun, but beneath the shade. [460] First then tell me who your family is.

Dionysus

I can tell you this easily, without boasting. I suppose you are familiar with flowery Tmolus.

Pentheus

I know of it; it surrounds the city of Sardis.

Dionysus

I am from there, and Lydia is my fatherland.

Pentheus

[465] Why do you bring these rites to Hellas?

Dionysus

Dionysus, the child of Zeus, sent me.

Pentheus

Is there a Zeus who breeds new gods there?

Dionysus

No, but the one who married Semele here.

Pentheus

Did he compel you at night, or in your sight?

Dionysus

[470] Seeing me just as I saw him, he gave me sacred rites.

Pentheus

What appearance do your rites have?

Dionysus

They can not be told to mortals uninitiated in Bacchic revelry.

Pentheus

And do they have any profit to those who sacrifice?

Dionysus

It is not lawful for you to hear, but they are worth knowing.

Pentheus

[475] You have counterfeited this well, so that I desire to hear.

Dionysus

The rites are hostile to whoever practices impiety.

Pentheus

Are you saying that you saw clearly what the god was like?

Dionysus

He was as he chose; I did not order this.

Pentheus

Again you diverted my question well, speaking mere nonsense.

Dionysus

[480] One will seem to be foolish if he speaks wisely to an ignorant man.

Pentheus

Did you come here first, bringing the god?

Dionysus

All the barbarians celebrate these rites.

Pentheus

Yes, for they are far more foolish than Hellenes.

Dionysus

In this at any rate they are wiser; but their laws are different.

Pentheus
[485] Do you perform the rites by night or by day?

Dionysus
Mostly by night; darkness conveys awe.

Pentheus
This is treacherous towards women, and unsound.

Dionysus
Even during the day someone may devise what is shameful.

Pentheus
You must pay the penalty for your evil contrivances.

Dionysus
[490] And you for your ignorance and impiety toward the god.

Pentheus
How bold the Bacchant is, and not unpracticed in speaking!

Dionysus
Tell me what I must suffer; what harm will you do to me?

Pentheus
First I will cut off your delicate hair.

Dionysus
My hair is sacred. I am growing it for the god.

Pentheus
[495] Next give me this thyrsos from your hands.

Dionysus
Take it from me yourself. I bear it as the ensign of Dionysus.

Pentheus
We will guard your body within, in prison.

Dionysus
The god himself will release me, whenever I want.

Pentheus
Yes, when you call him, standing among the Bacchae.

Dionysus
[500] Even now he see my sufferings from close by.

Pentheus
Where is he? He is not visible to my eyes.

Dionysus
Near me; but you, being impious, do not see him.

Pentheus
Toattendants
Seize him; he insults me and Thebes!

Dionysus
I warn you not to bind me, since I am in my senses and you are not.

Pentheus
[505] And I, more masterful than you, bid them to bind you.

Dionysus
You do not know why you live, or what you are doing, or who you are.

Pentheus
I am Pentheus, son of Echion and Agave.

Dionysus
You are well-suited to be miserable in your name.

Pentheus
Go.

Toattendants
Shut him up near the horse [510] stable, so that he may see only darkness.

ToDionysus
Dance there; and as for these women whom you have led here as accomplices to your crimes, we will either sell them or, stopping their hands from this noise and beating of skins, I will keep them as slaves at the loom.

Dionysus
[515] I will go, for I need not suffer that which is not necessary. But Dionysus, who you claim does not exist, will pursue you for these insults. For in injuring us, you put him in bonds.

Chorus

. . . Daughter of Achelous, [520] venerable Dirce, happy virgin, you once received the child of Zeus in your streams, when Zeus his father snatched him up from the immortal fire and saved him in his thigh, [525] crying out: "Go, Dithyrambus, enter this my male womb. I will make you illustrious, Bacchus, in Thebes, so that they will call you by this name." [530] But you, blessed Dirce, reject me with my garland-bearing company about you. Why do you refuse me, why do you flee me? I swear by the cluster-bearing [535] delight of Dionysus' vine that you will have a care for Bromius.

Chorus

What rage, what rage does the earth-born race show, and Pentheus, [540] once descended from a serpent—Pentheus, whom earth-born Echion bore, a fierce monster, not a mortal man, but like a bloody giant, hostile to the gods. [545] He will soon bind me, the hand-maid of Bromius, in chains, and he already holds my fellow-reveler within the house, hidden in a dark prison. [550] Do you see this, O Dionysus, son of Zeus, your priests in the dangers of restraint? Come, lord, down from Olympus, brandishing your golden thyrsos, [555] and restrain the insolence of the blood-thirsty man.

Chorus

Where on Nysa, which nourishes wild beasts, or on Corycian heights, do you lead with your thyrsos the bands of revelers? [560] Perhaps in the deep-wooded lairs of Olympus, where Orpheus once playing the lyre drew together trees by his songs, drew together the beasts of the fields. [565] Blessed Pieria, the Joyful one reveres you and will come to lead the dance in revelry; having crossed the swiftly flowing Axius he will bring the [570] whirling Maenads, leaving Lydias, giver of wealth to mortals, the father who they say fertilizes the land of beautiful horses with [575] fairest streams.

Dionysus

within

Io! Hear my voice, hear it, Io Bacchae, Io Bacchae!

Chorus

Who is here, who? From what quarter did the voice of the Joyful one summon me?

Dionysus

[580] Io! Io! I say again; it is I, the child of Zeus and Semele.

Chorus

Io! Io! Master, master! Come now to our company, Bromius.

Dionysus

[585] Shake the world's plain, lady Earthquake!

Chorus

Oh! Oh! Soon the palace of Pentheus will be shaken in ruin.

—Dionysus is in the halls. [590] Revere him.

—We revere him!

—Did you see these stone lintels on the pillars falling apart? Bromius cries out in victory indoors.

Dionysus

Light the fiery lamp of lightning! [595] Burn, burn Pentheus' home!

Chorus

Oh! Oh! Do you not see the the fire, do you not perceive, about the sacred tomb of Semele, the flame that Zeus' thunderbolt left? [600] Cast on the ground your trembling bodies, Maenads, cast them down, for our lord, Zeus' son, is coming against this palace, turning everything upside down.

Enter Dionysus

Dionysus

Barbarian women, have you fallen on the ground [605] so stricken with fear? You have, so it seems, felt Bacchus shaking the house of Pentheus. But get up and take courage, putting a stop to your trembling.

ChorusLeader

Oh greatest light for us in our joyful revelry, how happy I am to see you—I who was alone and desolate before.

Dionysus

[610] Did you despair when I was sent to fall into Pentheus' dark dungeon?

ChorusLeader

How not? Who was my guardian, if you met with misfortune? But how were you freed, having met with an impious man?

Dionysus

By myself I saved myself easily, without trouble.

ChorusLeader

[615] Did he not tie your hands in binding knots?

Dionysus

In this too I mocked him, for, thinking to bind me, he neither touched nor handled me, but fed on hope. He found a bull by the stable where he took and shut me up, and threw shackles around its knees and hooves, [620] breathing out fury, dripping sweat from his body, gnashing his teeth in his lips. But I, being near, sitting quietly, looked on. Meanwhile, Bacchus came and shook the house and kindled a flame on his mother's tomb. When Pentheus saw this, thinking that the house was burning, [625] he ran here and there, calling to the slaves to bring water, and every servant was at work, toiling in vain.

Then he let this labor drop, as I had escaped, and snatching a dark sword rushed into the house. Then Bromius, so it seems to me—I speak my opinion— [630] created a phantom in the courtyard. Pentheus rushed at it headlong, stabbing at the shining air, as though slaughtering me. Besides this, Bacchus inflicted other damage on him: he knocked his house to the ground, and everything was shattered into pieces, while he saw my bitter chains. From fatigue, [635] dropping his sword, he is exhausted. For he, a man, dared to join battle with a god. Now I have quietly left the house and come to you, with no thought of Pentheus.But I think—at any rate I hear the tramping of feet inside—he will soon come to the front of the house. What will he say after this? [640] I shall easily bear him, even if he comes boasting greatly. For it is the part of a wise man to practice restrained good temper.

Enter Pentheus

Penthcus

I have suffered terrible things; the stranger, who was recently constrained in bonds, has escaped me. Ah! [645] Here is the man. What is this? How do you appear in front of my house, having come out?

Dionysus

Stop, and put a stop to your anger.

Pentheus

How have you escaped your chains and come outside?

Dionysus

Did I not say—or did you not hear—that some one would deliver me?

Pentheus

[650] Who? You are always introducing strange explanations.

Dionysus

He who produces the rich-clustering vine for mortals.

Pentheus

<
*>

Dionysus

You reproach Dionysus for what is his glory.

Pentheus

I order you to close up all the towers around.

Dionysus

Why? Do gods not pass over walls too?

Pentheus

[655] You are wise, wise at least in all save what you should be wise in.

Dionysus

I was born wise in all that I should be.

Enter a messenger

Listen first to the words of this man, who has come from the mountain to bring you some message. I will await you, I will not try to escape.

Messenger

[660] Pentheus, ruler of this land of Thebes, I have come from Kithairon, where the bright flakes of white snow never melt.

Pentheus

What important news do you come to bring?

Messenger

Having seen the holy Bacchae, who [665] goaded to madness have darted from this land with their fair feet, I have come to tell you and the city, lord, that they are doing terrible things, beyond marvel. I wish to hear whether I should tell you in free speech the situation there or whether I should repress my report, [670] for I fear, lord, the quickness of your mood, your keen temper and your too imperious disposition.

Pentheus

Speak, as you will have immunity from me in any case. For it is not right to be angry with the just. The more you tell me terrible things about the Bacchae, [675] the more I will punish this one here who taught the women the

Messenger

The herds of grazing cattle were just climbing up the hill, at the time when the sun sends forth its rays, warming the earth. [680] I saw three companies of dancing women, one of which Autonoe led, the second your mother Agave, and the third Ino. All were asleep, their bodies relaxed, some resting their backs against pine foliage, [685] others laying their heads at random on the oak leaves, modestly, not as you say drunk with the goblet and the sound of the flute, hunting out Aphrodite through the woods in solitude. Your mother raised a cry, [690] standing up in the midst of the Bacchae, to wake their bodies from sleep, when she heard the lowing of the horned cattle. And they, casting off refreshing sleep from their eyes, sprang upright, a marvel of orderliness to behold, old, young, and still unmarried virgins. [695] First they let their hair loose over their shoulders, and secured their fawn-skins, as many of them as had released the fastenings of their knots, girding the dappled hides with serpents licking their jaws. And some, holding in their arms a gazelle or wild [700] wolf-pup, gave them white milk, as many as had abandoned their newborn infants and had their breasts still swollen. They put on garlands of ivy, and oak, and flowering yew. One took her thyrsos and struck it against a rock, [705] from which a dewy stream of water sprang forth. Another let her thyrsos strike the ground, and there the god sent forth a fountain of wine. All who desired the white drink scratched the earth with the tips of their fingers and obtained streams of milk; [710] and a sweet flow of honey dripped from their ivy thyrsoi; so that, had you been present and seen this, you would have approached with prayers the god whom you now blame. We herdsmen and shepherds gathered in order to [715] debate with one another concerning what strange and amazing things they were doing. Some one, a wanderer about the city and practised in speaking, said to us all: "You who inhabit the holy plains of the mountains, do you wish to hunt [720] Pentheus' mother Agave out from the Bacchic revelry and do the king a favor?" We thought he spoke well, and lay down in ambush, hiding ourselves in the foliage of bushes. They, at the appointed hour, began to wave the thyrsos in their revelries, [725] calling on Iacchus, the son of Zeus, Bromius, with united voice. The whole mountain revelled along with them and the beasts, and nothing was unmoved by their running. Agave happened to be leaping near me, and I sprang forth, wanting to snatch her, [730] abandoning the ambush where I had hidden myself. But she cried out: "O my fleet hounds, we are hunted by these men; but follow me! follow armed with your thyrsoi in your hands!" We fled and escaped [735] from being torn apart by the Bacchae, but they, with unarmed hands, sprang on the heifers browsing the grass. and you might see one rending asunder a fatted lowing calf, while others tore apart cows. [740] You might see ribs or cloven hooves tossed here and there; caught in the trees they dripped, dabbled in gore. Bulls who before were fierce, and showed their fury with their horns, stumbled to the ground, [745] dragged down by countless young hands. The garment of flesh was torn apart faster then you could blink your royal eyes. And like birds raised in their course, they proceeded along the level plains, which by the streams of the Asopus [750] produce the bountiful Theban crop. And falling like soldiers upon Hysiae and Erythrae, towns situated below the rock of Kithairon, they turned everything upside down. They were snatching children from their homes; [755] and whatever they put on their shoulders, whether bronze or iron, was not held on by bonds, nor did it fall to the ground. They carried fire on their locks, but it did not burn them. Some people in rage took up arms, being plundered by the Bacchae, [760] and the sight of this was terrible to behold, lord. For their pointed spears drew no blood, but the women, hurling the thyrsoi from their hands, kept wounding them and turned them to flight—women did this to men, not without the help of some god. [765] And they returned where they had come from, to the very fountains which the god had sent forth for them, and washed off the blood, and snakes cleaned the drops from the women's cheeks with their tongues. Receive this god then, whoever he is, [770] into this city, master. For he is great in other respects, and they say this too of him, as I hear, that he gives to mortals the vine that puts an end to grief. Without wine there is no longer Aphrodite or any other pleasant thing for men.

ChorusLeader

[775] I fear to speak freely to the king, but I will speak nevertheless: Dionysus is inferior to none of the gods.

Pentheus

Already like fire does this insolence of the Bacchae blaze up, a great reproach for the Hellenes. [780] But we must not hesitate. Go to the Electran gates, bid all the shield-bearers and riders of swift-footed horses to assemble, as well as all who brandish the light shield and pluck bowstrings with their hands, so that we can make an assault against [785] the Bacchae. For it is indeed too much if we suffer what we are suffering at the hands of women.

Dionysus

Pentheus, though you hear my words, you obey not at all. Though I suffer ill at your hands, still I say that it is not right for you to raise arms against a god, [790] but to remain calm. Bromius will not allow you to remove the Bacchae from the joyful mountains.

Pentheus

Do not instruct me, but be content in your escape from prison. Or shall I bring punishment upon you again?

Dionysus

I would sacrifice to the god rather [795] than kick against his spurs in anger, a mortal against a god.

Pentheus

I will sacrifice, making a great slaughter of the women, as they deserve, in the glens of Kithairon.

Dionysus

You will all flee. And it will be a source of shame that you turn your bronze shields away from the thyrsoi of the Bacchae.

Pentheus

[800] This stranger with whom I am locked together is impossible, and neither suffering nor doing will he be quiet.

Dionysus

My friend, there is still opportunity to arrange these things well.

Pentheus

Doing what? Being a slave to my slaves?

Dionysus

Without weapons I will bring the women here.

Pentheus

[805] Alas! You are contriving this as a trick against me.

Dionysus

What sort, if I wish to save you by my contrivances?

Pentheus

You have devised this together, so that you may have your revelry forever.

Dionysus
I certainly did—that is so—with the god.

Pentheus
To a servant
Bring me my armor. *To Dionysus* And you, stop speaking.

Dionysus
[810] Ah! Do you wish to see them sitting together in the mountains?

Pentheus
Certainly. I'd give an enormous amount of gold for that.

Dionysus
Why do you desire this so badly?

Pentheus
I would be sorry to see them in their drunkenness.

Dionysus
[815] But would you see gladly what is grievous to you?

Pentheus
To be sure, sitting quietly under the pines.

Dionysus
But they will track you down, even if you go in secret.

Pentheus
You are right: I will go openly.

Dionysus
Shall I guide you? Will you attempt the journey?

Pentheus
[820] Lead me as quickly as possible. I grudge you the time.

Dionysus
Put linen clothes on your body then.

Pentheus
What is this? Shall I then, instead of a man, be reckoned among the women?

Dionysus
Lest they kill you if you are seen there as a man.

Pentheus
Again you speak correctly: how wise you have been all along!

Dionysus
[825] Dionysus taught me these things fully.

Pentheus
How can your advice to me be well carried out?

Dionysus
I will go inside and dress you.

Pentheus
In what clothing? Female? But shame holds me back.

Dionysus
Are you no longer eager to view the maenads?

Pentheus
[830] What clothing do you bid me to put on my body?

Dionysus
I will spread out hair at length on your head.

Pentheus
What is the second part of my outfit?

Dionysus
A robe down to your feet. And you will wear a headband.

Pentheus
And what else will you add to this for me?

Dionysus
[835] A thyrsos in your hand, and a dappled fawn-skin.

Pentheus
I could not put on a woman's dress.

Dionysus
But you will shed blood if you join battle with the Bacchae.

Pentheus

True. We must go first and spy.

Dionysus

This is at any rate wiser than hunting trouble with trouble.

Pentheus

[840] And how will I go through the city without being seen by the Thebans?

Dionysus

We will go on deserted roads. I will lead you.

Pentheus

Anything is better than to be mocked by the Bacchae. We two will go into the house . . . and I will consider what seems best.

Dionysus

It will be so; in any case I am ready.

Pentheus

[845] I will go in. For either I will go bearing arms, or I will obey your counsels.

Dionysus

Women, the man is caught in our net. He will go to the Bacchae, where he will pay the penalty with his death. Dionysus, now it is your job; for you are not far off. [850] Let us punish him. First drive him out of his wits, send upon him a dizzying madness, since if he is of sound mind he will not consent to wear women's clothing, but driven out of his senses he will put it on. I want him to be a source of laughter to the Thebans, led through the city in [855] women's guise after making such terrible threats in the past. But now I will go to fit on Pentheus the dress he will wear to the house of Hades, slaughtered by his mother's hands. He will recognize the son of Zeus, [860] Dionysus, who is in fact a god, the most terrible and yet most mild to men.

Chorus

Shall I move my white foot in the night-long dance, aroused to a frenzy, [865] throwing my head to the dewy air, like a fawn sporting in the green pleasures of the meadow, when it has escaped a fearful chase beyond the watchers [870] over the well-woven nets, and the hunter hastens his dogs on their course with his call, while she, with great exertion and a storm-swift running, rushes along the plain by the river, rejoicing [875] in the solitude apart from men and in the thickets of the shady-foliaged woods.

What is wisdom? Or what greater honor do the gods give to mortals than to hold one's hand [880] in strength over the head of enemies? What is good is always dear.

Chorus

Divine strength is roused with difficulty, but still is sure. It chastises those mortals [885] who honor folly and those who in their insanity do not extol the gods. The gods cunningly conceal the long pace of time and [890] hunt the impious. For it is not right to determine or plan anything beyond the laws. For it is a light expense to hold that whatever is divine has power, [895] and that which has been law for a long time is eternal and has its origin in nature.

What is wisdom? Or what greater honor do the gods give to mortals than to hold one's hand [900] in strength over the head of enemies? What is good is always dear.

Chorus

Happy is he [1] who has fled a storm on the sea, and reached harbor. Happy too is he who has overcome his hardships. [905] One surpass another in different ways, in wealth or power. There are innumerable hopes to innumerable men, and some result in wealth to mortals, while others fail. [910] But I call him blessed whose life is happy day to day.

Dionysus

You who are eager to see what you ought not and hasty in pursuit of what ought not to be pursued—I mean you, Pentheus, come forth before the house, be seen by me, [915] wearing the clothing of a woman, of an inspired maenad, a spy upon your mother and her company.

Pentheus emerges.
In appearance you are like one of Kadmos' daughters.

Pentheus

Oh look! I think I see two suns, and twin Thebes, the seven-gated city. [920] And you seem to lead me, being like a bull and horns seem to grow on your head. But were you ever before a beast? For you have certainly now become a bull.

Dionysus

The god accompanies us, now at truce with us, though formerly not propitious. Now you see what you should see.

Pentheus

[925] How do I look? Don't I have the posture of Ino, or of my mother Agave?

Dionysus

Looking at you I think I see them. But this lock of your hair has come out of place, not the way I arranged it under your headband.

Pentheus

[930] I displaced it indoors, shaking my head forwards and backwards and practising my Bacchic revelry.

Dionysus

But I who ought to wait on you will re-arrange it. Hold up your head.

Pentheus

Here, you arrange it; for I depend on you, indeed.

Dionysus

[935] Your girdle has come loose, and the pleats of your gown do not extend regularly down around your ankles.

Pentheus

At least on my right leg, I believe they don't. But on this side the robe sits well around the back of my leg.

Dionysus

You will surely consider me the best of your friends, [940] when contrary to your expectation you see the Bacchae acting modestly.

Pentheus

But shall I be more like a maenad holding the thyrsos in my right hand, or in my left?

Dionysus

You must hold it in your right hand and raise your right foot in unison with it. I praise you for having changed your mind.

Pentheus

[945] Could I carry on my shoulders the glens of Kithairon, Bacchae and all?

Dionysus

You could if you were willing. The state of mind you had before was unsound, but now you think as you ought.

Pentheus

Shall we bring levers? Or shall I draw them up with my hands, [950] putting a shoulder or arm under the mountain-tops?

Dionysus

But don't destroy the seats of the Nymphs and the places where Pan plays his pipes.

Pentheus

Well said. The women are not to be taken by force; I will hide in the pines.

Dionysus

[955] You will hide yourself as you should be hidden, coming as a crafty spy on the Maenads.

Pentheus

Oh, yes! I imagine that like birds they are in the bushes held in the sweetest grips of love.

Dionysus

You have been sent as a guard against this very event. [960] Perhaps you will catch them, if you yourself are not caught before.

Pentheus

Bring me through the midst of the Theban land. I am the only man of them who dares to perform this deed.

Dionysus

You alone bear the burden for this city, you alone. Therefore the labors which are proper await you. [965] Follow me. I am your saving guide: another will lead you down from there.

Pentheus

Yes, my mother.

Dionysus

And you will be remarkable to all.

Pentheus

I am going for this reason.

Dionysus

You will return here being carried—

Pentheus
You talk of a delicacy for me.

Dionysus
In the arms of your mother.

Pentheus
You will force me to luxury.

Dionysus
[970] Yes indeed, such luxury!

Pentheus
I will get what I deserve.

Dionysus
You are terrible, terrible, and you go to terrible sufferings, so that you will find a renown reaching to heaven. Reach out your hands, Agave, and you too, her sisters, daughters of Kadmos. I lead this young man [975] to a great contest, and Bromius and I will be the victors. The rest the matter itself will show.

Chorus
Go to the mountain, go, fleet hounds of Madness, where the daughters of Kadmos hold their company, and drive them raving [980] against the mad spy on the Maenads, the one dressed in women's attire. His mother will be the first to see him from a smooth rock or crag, as he lies in ambush, and she will cry out to the maenads: [985] "Who is this seeker of the mountain-going Kadmeans who has come to the mountain, to the mountain, Bacchae? Who bore him? For he was not born from a woman's blood, but is the offspring of some lioness [990] or of Libyan Gorgons. Let manifest justice go forth, let it go with sword in hand, slaying through the throat [995] this godless, lawless, unjust, earth-born offspring of Echion.

Chorus
Whoever with wicked mind and unjust rage regarding your rites, Bacchus, and those of your mother, comes with raving heart [1000] and mad disposition violently to overcome by force what is invincible—death is the discipline for his purposes, accepting no excuses when the affairs of the gods are concerned; to act like a mortal—this is a life that is free from pain. [1005] I do not envy wisdom, but rejoice in hunting it. But other things are great and manifest. Oh, for life to flow towards the good, to be pure and pious day and night, and to honor the gods, [1010] banishing customs that are outside of justice.Let

manifest justice go forth, let it go with sword in hand, slaying through the throat [1015] this godless, lawless, unjust, earth-born offspring of Echion.

Chorus

Appear as a bull or many-headed serpent or raging lion to see. [1020] Go, Bacchus, with smiling face throw a deadly noose around the hunter of the Bacchae as he falls beneath the flock of Maenads.

SecondMessenger

Oh house once fortunate in Hellas, [1025] house of the Sidonian old man who once sowed in the ground the earth-born harvest of the serpent Ophis, how I groan for you, though I am a slave, but still [the masters' affairs are a concern to good servants].[1].

ChorusLeader

What is it? Do you bring some news from the Bacchae?

Messenger

[1030] Pentheus, the child of Echion, is dead.

sung

Chorus

Leader

Lord Bacchus, truly you appear to be a great god.

Messenger

What do you mean? Why have you said this? Do you rejoice at the misfortunes of my master, woman?

ChorusLeader

I, a foreign woman, rejoice with foreign songs; [1035] for no longer do I cower in fear of chains.

Messenger

Do you think Thebes so lacking in men?

sung

ChorusLeader

Dionysus, Dionysus, not Thebes, holds my allegiance.

Messenger

You may be forgiven, but still it is not good [1040] to rejoice at troubles once they have actually taken place, women.

ChorusLeader

Tell me, speak, what kind of a death did he die, the unjust man who did unjust things?

Messenger

When we left the dwellings of the Theban land and crossed the streams of Asopus, [1045] we began to ascend the heights of Kithairon, Pentheus and I—for I was following my master—and the stranger who was our guide to the sight. First we sat in a grassy vale, [1050] keeping our feet and voices quiet, so that we might see them without being seen. There was a little valley surounded by precipices, irrigated with streams, shaded by pine trees, where the Maenads were sitting, their hands busy with delightful labors. Some of them were crowning again [1055] the worn thyrsos, making it leafy with ivy, while some, like colts freed from the painted yoke, were singing a Bacchic melody to one another. And the unhappy Pentheus said, not seeing the crowd of women: "Stranger, [1060] from where we are standing I cannot see these false Maenads. But on the hill, ascending a lofty pine, I might view properly the shameful acts of the Maenads."And then I saw the stranger perform a marvelous deed. For seizing hold of the lofty top-most branch of the pine tree, [1065] he pulled it down, pulled it, pulled it to the dark earth. It was bent just as a bow or a curved wheel, when it is marked out by a compass, describes a circular course [1]: in this way the stranger drew the mountain bough with his hands and bent it to the earth, doing no mortal's deed. [1070] He sat Pentheus down on the pine branch, and let it go upright through his hands steadily, taking care not to shake him off. The pine stood firmly upright into the sky, with my master seated on its back. [1075] He was seen by the Maenads more than he saw them, for sitting on high he was all but apparent, and the stranger was no longer anywhere to be seen, when a voice, Dionysus as I guess, cried out from the air: "Young women, [1080] I bring the one who has made you and me and my rites a laughing-stock. Now punish him!" And as he said this a light of holy fire was placed between heaven and earth. The air became quiet and the woody glen [1085] kept its leaves silent, nor would you have heard the sounds of animals. But they, not having heard the sound clearly, stood upright and looked all around. He repeated his order, and when the daughters of Kadmos recognized the clear command of Bacchus, [1090] they rushed forth, swift as a dove, running with eager speed of feet, his mother Agave, and her sisters, and all the Bacchae. They leapt through the torrent-streaming valley and mountain cliffs, frantic with the inspiration of the god. [1095] When they saw my master sitting in the pine, first they climbed a rock towering opposite the tree and began to hurl at him boulders violently thrown. Some aimed with pine branches and other women hurled their thyrsoi through the air [1100] at Pentheus, a sad target indeed. But they did not reach him, for the wretched man, caught with no way out, sat at a height too great for their eagerness. Finally like lightning they smashed oak branches and began to tear up the roots of the tree with ironless levers. [1105] When they did not succeed in their toils, Agave said: "Come, standing round in a circle, each seize a branch, Maenads, so that we may catch the beast who has climbed aloft, and so that he does not make public the secret dances of the god." They applied countless hands [1110] to the pine and dragged it up from the earth. Pentheus fell crashing to the ground from his lofty seat, wailing greatly: for he knew he was in terrible trouble.His mother, as priestess, began the slaughter, [1115] and fell upon him. He threw the headband from his head so that the wretched Agave might recognize and not kill him. Touching her cheek, he said: "It is I, mother, your son, Pentheus, whom you bore in the house of Echion. [1120] Pity me, mother, and do not kill me, your child, for my sins."But she, foaming at the mouth and twisting her eyes all about, not thinking as she ought, was possessed by Bacchus, and he did not persuade her. [1125] Seizing his left arm at the elbow and propping her foot against the unfortunate man's side, she tore out his shoulder, not by her own strength, but the god gave facility to her hands. Ino began to work on the other side, [1130] tearing his flesh, while Autonoe and the whole crowd of the Bacchae pressed on. All were making noise together, he groaning as much as he had life left in him, while they shouted in victory. One of them bore his arm, another a foot, boot and all. His ribs were stripped bare [1135] from their tearings. The whole band, hands bloodied, were playing a game of catch with Pentheus' flesh.His body lies in different places, part under the rugged rocks, part in the deep foliage of the woods, not easy to be sought. His miserable head, [1140] which his mother happened to take in her hands, she fixed on the end of a thyrsos and carries through the midst of Kithairon like that of a savage lion, leaving her sisters among the Maenads' dances. She is coming inside these walls, preening herself [1145] on the ill-fated prey, calling Bacchus her fellow hunter, her accomplice in the chase, the glorious victor—in whose service she wins a triumph of tears.And as for me, I will depart out of the way of this calamity before Agave reaches the house. [1150] Soundness of mind and reverence for the affairs of the gods is best; and this, I think, is the wisest possession for those mortals

Chorus

Let us honor Bacchus with the dance, let us raise a shout for what has befallen [1155] Pentheus, descendant of the serpent, who assumed female attire and the wand, the beautiful thyrsos—certain death—and a bull was the leader of his calamity. [1160] Kadmean Bacchae, you have accomplished a glorious victory, but one that brings woe and tears. It is a noble contest to cover one's dripping hands with the blood of one's own son.o adopt it.

ChorusLeader

[1165] But, for I see Pentheus' mother Agave coming home, her eyes contorted, receive the revel of the god of joy!

EnterAgave

Agave
Asian Bacchae—

Chorus
Why do you excite me, oh?

Agave
I am bringing home from the mountain a [1170] freshly cut tendril to the house, blessed prey.

Chorus
I see it and will accept you as a fellow reveler.

Agave
I caught this young wild lion cub without snares, [1175] as you can see.

Chorus
From what desert?

Agave
Kithairon—

Chorus
Kithairon?

Agave
slew him.

Chorus
Who struck him?

Agave
The honor is mine first. [1180] I am called blessed Agave in the revels.

Chorus
Who else?

Agave
Kadmos'—

Chorus
Kadmos' what?

Agave
His other offspring took hold of this beast after me, after me. This is a lucky catch!

Chorus

Agave
Share in the feast then.

Chorus
What? I share in the feast, wretched woman?

Agave
[1185] The bull is young; his cheek is just growing downy under his soft-haired crest.

Chorus
Yes, his hair looks like a wild beast's.

Agave
Bacchus, a wise huntsman, [1190] wisely set the Maenads against this beast.

Chorus
Our lord is a hunter.

Agave
Do you praise me?

Chorus
I praise you.

Agave
Soon the Kadmeans—

Chorus
[1195] And your son Pentheus, too—

Agave
Will praise his mother who has caught this lion-like prey.

Chorus
Extraordinary.

Agave
And extraordinarily caught.

Chorus
Are you proud?

Agave
I am delighted, for I have performed great—yes, great—and notable deeds on this hunt.

Choruseader
[1200] Now show the citizens, wretched woman, the booty which you have brought in victory.

Agave
You who dwell in this fair-towered city of the Theban land, come to see this prey which we the daughters of Kadmos hunted down, [1205] not with thonged Thessalian javelins, or with nets, but with the fingers of our white arms. And then should huntsmen boast and use in vain the work of spear-makers? But we caught and [1210] tore apart the limbs of this beast with our very own hands. Where is my old father? Let him approach. And where is my son Pentheus? Let him take a ladder and raise its steps against the house so that he can fasten to the triglyphs this [1215] lion's head which I have captured and brought here.

Enter Kadmos and his servants, carrying the remains of Pentheus' body

Kadmos
Follow me, carrying the miserable burden of Pentheus, follow me, slaves, before the house; exhausted from countless searches, I am bringing his body, for I discovered it in the folds of Kithairon, [1220] torn apart; I picked up nothing in the same place, and it was lying in the woods where discovery was

difficult. For some one told me of my daughters' bold deeds, when I had already come within the walls of the city on my return from the Bacchae with old Teiresias. [1225] I turned back to the mountain and now bring here my child who was killed by the Maenads. For I saw Autonoe, who once bore Actaeon to Aristaeus, and Ino with her, still mad in the thicket, wretched creatures. [1230] But some one told me that Agave was coming here with Bacchic foot, and this was correct, for I see her—no happy sight!

Agave

Father, you may make a great boast, that you have born daughters the best by far of all [1235] mortals. I mean all of us, but myself especially, who have left my shuttle at the loom and gone on to greater things, to catch wild animals with my two hands. And having taken him, I carry these spoils of honor in my arms, as you see, [1240] so that they may hang from your house. You father, receive them in your hands. Preening yourself in my catch, call your friends to a feast. For you are blessed, blessed, now that we have performed these deeds.

Kadmos

O grief beyond measuring, one which I cannot stand to see, [1245] that you have performed murder with miserable hands. Having cast down a fine sacrificial victim to the gods, you invite Thebes and me to a banquet. Alas, first for your troubles, then for my own. How justly, yet too severely, [1250] lord Bromius the god has destroyed us, though he is a member of our own family.

Agave

How morose and sullen in its countenance is man's old age! I hope that my son is a good hunter, taking after his mother's ways, when he goes after wild beasts [1255] together with the young men of Thebes. But all he can do is fight with the gods. You must admonish him, father. Who will call him here to my sight, so that he may see how lucky I am?

Kadmos

Alas, alas! When you realize what you have done [1260] you will suffer a terrible pain. But if you remain forever in the state you are in now, though hardly fortunate, you will not imagine that you are unfortunate.

Agave

But what of these matters is not right, or what is painful?

Kadmos

First cast your eye up to this sky.

Agave

[1265] All right; why do you tell me to look at it?

Kadmos

Is it still the same, or does it appear to have changed?

Agave

It is brighter than before and more translucent.

Kadmos

Is your soul still quivering?

Agave

I don't understand your words. I have become somehow [1270] sobered, changing from my former state of mind.

Kadmos

Can you hear and respond clearly?

Agave

Yes, for I forget what we said before, father.

Kadmos

To whose house did you come in marriage?

Agave

You gave me, as they say, to Echion, the sown man.

Kadmos

[1275] What son did you bear to your husband in the house?

Agave

Pentheus, from my union with his father.

Kadmos

Whose head do you hold in your hands?

Agave

A lion's, as they who hunted him down said.

Kadmos

Examine it correctly then; it takes but little effort to see.

Agave

[1280] Ah! What do I see? What is this that I carry in my hands?

Kadmos

Look at it and learn more clearly.

Agave

I see the greatest grief, wretched that I am.

Kadmos

Does it seem to you to be like a lion?

Agave

No, but I, wretched, hold the head of Pentheus.

Kadmos

[1285] Yes, much lamented before you recognized him.

Agave

Who killed him? How did he come into my hands?

Kadmos

Miserable truth, how inopportunely you arrive!

Agave

Tell me. My heart leaps at what is to come.

Kadmos

You and your sisters killed him.

Agave

[1290] Where did he die? Was it here at home, or in what place?

Kadmos

Where formerly dogs divided Actaeon among themselves.

Agave

And why did this ill-fated man go to Kithairon?

Kadmos

He went to mock the god and your revelry.

Agave

But in what way did we go there?

Kadmos

[1295] You were mad, and the whole city was frantic with Bacchus.

Agave

Dionysus destroyed us—now I understand.

Kadmos

Being insulted with insolence, for you did not consider him a god.

Agave

And where is the body of my dearest child, father?

Kadmos

I have traced it with difficulty and brought it back.

Agave

[1300] Are its joints laid properly together?

Kadmos

<
*>

Agave

What part did Pentheus have in my folly?

Kadmos

He, like you, did not revere the god, who therefore joined all in one ruin, both you and this one here, and thus destroyed the house and me, [1305] , who am bereft of my male children and see this offspring of your womb, wretched woman, most miserably and shamefully slain. He was the hope of our line— you, child, who supported the house, son of my daughter, [1310] an object of fear to the city; seeing you, no one wished to insult the old man, for you would have given a worthy punishment. But now I, great Kadmos, who sowed and reaped [1315] a most glorious crop, the Theban people, will be banished from the house without honor. Dearest of men—for though you are dead I still count you among my dearest, child—no longer will you embrace me, calling me grandfather, touching my chin with your hand, child, and [1320] saying: "Who wrongs you, old man, who dishonors you? Who vexes and troubles your heart? Tell me, father, so that I can punish the one who does you wrong." But now I am miserable, while you are wretched, your mother is pitiful, and wretched too are your relatives. [1325] If anyone scorns the gods, let him look to the death of this man and acknowledge them.

ChorusLeader

I grieve for you, Kadmos. Your daughter's child has a punishment deserved indeed, but grievous to you.

Agave

Father, for you see how much my situation has changed ...

To Kadmos

Dionysus

[1330] ... changing your form, you will become a dragon, and your wife, Harmonia, Ares' daughter, whom you though mortal held in marriage, will be turned into a beast, and will receive in exchange the form of a serpent. And as the oracle of Zeus says, you will drive along with your wife a chariot of heifers, ruling over barbarians. [1335] You will sack many cities with a force of countless numbers. And when they plunder the oracle of Apollo, they will have a miserable return, but Ares will protect you and Harmonia and will settle your life in the land of the blessed. [1340] That is what I, Dionysus, born not from a mortal father, but from Zeus, say. And if you had known how to be wise when you did not wish to be, you would have acquired Zeus' son as an ally, and would now be happy.

Kadmos

Dionysus, we beseech you, we have acted injustly.

Dionysus

[1345] You have learned it too late; you did not know it when you should have.

Kadmos

Now we know, but you go too far against us.

Dionysus

Yes, for I, a god by birth, was insulted by you.

Kadmos

Gods should not resemble mortals in their anger.

Dionysus

My father Zeus approved this long ago.

Agave

[1350] Alas! A miserable exile has been decreed for us, old man.

Dionysus

Why then do you delay what must necessarily be?

Kadmos

Child, what a terrible disaster we have all come to—unhappy you, your sisters, and unhappy me. I shall reach a foreign land [1355] as an aged immigrant. Still it is foretold that I shall bring into Hellas a motley barbarian army. Leading their spears, I, having the fierce nature of a serpent, will bring my wife Harmonia, daughter of Ares, to the altars and tombs of Hellas. [1360] I will neither rest from my troubles in my misery, nor will I sail over the downward flowing Acheron and be at peace.

Agave

O father, I will go into exile deprived of you.

Kadmos

Why do you embrace me with your hands, child, [1365] like a swan for its exhausted gray-haired parent?

Agave

For where can I turn, banished from my father-land?

Kadmos

I do not know, child; your father is a poor ally.

Agave

Farewell, house, farewell, city of my forefathers. In misfortune I leave you, [1370] a fugitive from my chamber.

Kadmos

Go now, child, to the land of Aristaeus

Agave

I grieve for you, father.

Kadmos

And I for you, child, and I weep for your sisters.

Agave

Terribly indeed has [1375] lord Dionysus brought this misery to your home.

Dionysus

Yes, for I suffered terrible things at your hands, with my name not honored in Thebes.

Agave

Farewell, my father.

Kadmos

Farewell, unhappy [1380] daughter; and yet you cannot easily fare well.

Agave

Lead me, escorts, where I may take my pitiful sisters as companions to my exile. May I go where accursed Kithairon may not see me, [1385] nor I see Kithairon with my eyes, nor where a memorial of a thyrsos has been dedicated; let these concern other Bacchae.

Chorus

Many are the forms of divine things, and the gods bring to pass many things unexpectedly; [1390] what is expected has not been accomplished, but the god has found out a means for doing things unthought of. So too has this event turned out.

HOMERIC HYMNS[211]

I. TO DIONYSUS

[1] ... For some say, at Dracanum; and some, on windy Icarus; and some, in Naxos, O Heaven-born, Insewn; and others by the deep-eddying river Alpheus that pregnant Semele bare you to Zeus the thunder-lover. [5] And others yet, lord, say you were born in Thebes; but all these lie. The Father of men and gods gave you birth remote from men and secretly from white-armed Hera. There is a certain Nysa, a mountain most high and richly grown with woods, far off in Phoenice, near the streams of Aegyptus ...

[10] "and men will lay up for her many offerings in her shrines. And as these things are three, so shall mortals ever sacrifice perfect hecatombs to you at your feasts each three years."

The Son of Cronos spoke and nodded with his dark brows. And the divine locks of the king flowed forward [15] from his immortal head, and he made great Olympus reel. So spake wise Zeus and ordained it with a nod.

Be favorable, O Insewn, Inspirer of frenzied women! we singers sing of you as we begin and as we end a strain, and none forgetting you may call holy

---

211 The Homeric Hymns and Homerica with an English Translation by Hugh G. Evelyn-White. Homeric Hymns. Cambridge, MA., Harvard University Press; London, William Heinemann Ltd. 1914.

song to mind. [20] And so, farewell, Dionysus, Insewn, with your mother Semele whom men call Thyone.

XXVI. TO DIONYSUS

[1] I begin to sing of ivy-crowned Dionysus, the loud-crying god, splendid son of Zeus and glorious Semele. The rich-haired Nymphs received him in their bosoms from the lord his father and fostered and nurtured him carefully [5] in the dells of Nysa, where by the will of his father he grew up in a sweet-smelling cave, being reckoned among the immortals. But when the goddesses had brought him up, a god oft hymned, then began he to wander continually through the woody coombes, thickly wreathed with ivy and laurel. And the Nymphs followed in his train [10] with him for their leader; and the boundless forest was filled with their outcry.

And so hail to you, Dionysus, god of abundant clusters! Grant that we may come again rejoicing to this season, and from that season onwards for many a year.

ORPHIC HYMNS

XXIX. TO BACCHUS [DIONYSOS]

The Fumigation from Storax.

Bacchus [Dionysos] I call, loud-sounding and divine, fanatic God, a two-fold shape is thine:

Thy various names and attributes I sing, O, first-born, thrice begotten, Bacchic king:

Rural, ineffable, two-form'd, obscure, two-horn'd, with ivy crown'd, euion, pure.

Bull-fac'd, and martial, bearer of the vine, endu'd with counsel prudent [Eubouleos] and divine:

Triennial, whom the leaves of vines adorn, of Jove [Zeus] and Proserpine [Persephoneia], occultly born.

Immortal dæmon, hear my suppliant voice, give me in blameless plenty to rejoice;

And listen gracious to my mystic pray'r, surrounded with thy choir of nurses fair.

XLIII. TO SEMELE

The Fumigation from Storax.
Cadmean Goddess, universal queen, thee, Semele I call, of beauteous mien;
Deep-bosom'd, lovely flowing locks are thine, mother of Bacchus [Dionysos], joyful and divine,
The mighty offspring, whom love's thunder bright, forc'd immature, and fright'ned into light:
Born from the deathless counsels, secret, high, of Jove Saturnian [Zeus Kronion], regent of the sky
Whom Proserpine [Persephone] permits to view the light, and visit mortals from the realms of night:
Constant attending on the sacred rites, and feast triennial, which thy soul delights;
When thy son's wond'rous birth mankind relate, and secrets deep, and holy celebrate.
Now I invoke thee, great Cadmean queen, to bless these rites with countenance serene.

XLIV. TO DIONYSIUS BASSAREUS TRIENNALIS

A Hymn
Come, blessed Dionysius [Dionysos], various nam'd, bull-fac'd,
begot from Thunder, Bacchus [Bakkhos] fam'd.
Bassarian God, of universal might, whom swords, and blood, and sacred rage delight:
In heav'n rejoicing, mad, loud-sounding God, furious inspirer, bearer of the rod:
By Gods rever'd, who dwell'st with human kind, propitious come, with much-rejoicing mind.

XLV. TO LIKNITUS BACCHUS [LIKNITOS DIONYSOS]

The Fumigation from Manna.
Liknitan Bacchus [Liknitos Dionysos], bearer of the vine, thee I invoke to bless these rites divine:
Florid and gay, of nymphs the blossom bright, and of fair Venus [Aphrodite], Goddess of delight,
'Tis thine mad footsteps with mad nymphs to beat, dancing thro' groves with lightly leaping feet:

From Jove's [Zeus'] high counsels nurst by Proserpine [Persephoneia],
and born the dread of all the pow'rs divine:
Come, blessed pow'r, regard thy suppliant's voice, propitious come, and
in these rites rejoice.

XLVI. TO BACCHUS PERICIONIUS [DIONYSOS PERIKIONIOS]

The Fumigation from Aromatics.
Bacchus Pericionius [Dionysos Perikionios], hear my pray'r,
who mad'st the house of Cadmus once thy care,
With matchless force, his pillars twining round, (when burning thunders
shook the solid ground,
In flaming, founding torrents borne along), propt by thy grasp indissolu-
bly strong.
Come mighty Bacchus to these rites inclin'd, and bless thy suppliants
with rejoicing mind.

XLVII. TO SABASIUS [ZABAZIOS]

The Fumigation from Aromatics.
Hear me, illustrious father, dæmon fam'd.
Great Saturn's [Kronos'] offspring, and Sabasius [Zabazios] nam'd;
Inserting Bacchus, bearer of the vine, and founding God, within thy thigh
divine,
That when mature, the Dionysian God might burst the bands of his con-
ceal'd abode,
And come to sacred Tmolus, his delight, where Ippa dwells, all beautiful
and bright.
Come blessed Phrygian God, the king of all, and aid thy mystics, when on
thee they call.

XLVIII. TO IPPA

The Fumigation from Storax.
Great nurse of Bacchus [Bakkhos], to my pray'r incline, for holy Sabus'
secret rites are thine,
The mystic rites of Bacchus' nightly choirs, compos'd of sacred, loud-re-
sounding fires:
Hear me, terrestrial mother, mighty queen, whether on Phyrgia's holy
mountain seen,

Or if to dwell in Tmolus thee delights, with holy aspect come, and bless these rites.

XLIX. TO LYSIUS LENÆUS [LYSIOS LENAIOS]

A Hymn.

Hear me, Jove's [Zeus'] son, blest Bacchus, God of wine, born of two mothers, honor'd and divine;

Lysian, Euion Bacchus, various-nam'd, of Gods the offspring secret, holy, fam'd:

Fertile and nourishing whose liberal care earth's fruits increases, flourishing and fair;

Sounding, magnanimous, Lenæan pow'r, O various form'd, medic'nal, holy flow'r:

Mortals in thee, repose from labour find, delightful charm, desir'd by all mankind:

Fair-hair'd Euion, Bromian, joyful God, Lysian, invested with the leafy rod.

To these our rites, benignant pow'r incline, when fav'ring men, or when on Gods you shine;

Be present to thy mystic's suppliant pray'r, rejoicing come, and fruits abundant bear.

LI. TO TRIETERICUS [TRIETERIKOS]

The Fumigation from Aromatics.

Bacchus fanatic, much-nam'd, blest, divine, bull-fac'd Lenæan, bearer of the vine;

From fire descended, raging, Nysian king, from whom initial ceremonies spring:

Liknitan Bacchus, pure and fiery bright, prudent [Eubouleos], crown-bearer, wandering in the night;

Pupil of Proserpine, mysterious pow'r, triple, ineffable, Jove's [Zeus'] secret flow'r:

Ericapæus, first-begotten nam'd, of Gods the father, and the offspring fam'd:

Bearing a sceptre, leader of the choir, whose dancing feet, fanatic Furies fire,

When the triennial band thou dost inspire.

Loud-sounding, Tages, of a fiery light, born of two mothers, Amphietus bright:

Wand'ring on mountains, cloth'd with skins of deer, Apollo, golden-ray'd, whom all revere.

God of the grape with leaves of ivy crown'd, Bassarian, lovely, virgin-like, renown'd

Come blessed pow'r, regard thy mystics voice, propitious come, and in these rites rejoice.

LII. TO AMPHIETUS BACCHUS [AMPHIETOS BAKKHOS]

The Fumigation from every Aromatic except Frankincense.

Terrestrial Dionysius [Dionysos Khthonios], hear my pray'r, awak'ned rise with nymphs of lovely hair:

Great Amphietus Bacchus, annual God, who laid asleep in Proserpine's [Persephone's] abode,

Did'st lull to drowsy and oblivious rest, the rites triennial, and the sacred feast;

Which rous'd again by thee, in graceful ring, thy nurses round thee mystic anthems sing;

When briskly dancing with rejoicing pow'rs, thou mov'st in concert with the circling hours.

Come, blessed, fruitful, horned, and divine, and on these rites with joyful aspect shine;

Accept the general incense and the pray'r, and make prolific holy fruits thy care.

APPENDIX - ILLUSTRATIONS

Dionysos thiasos, Attic red figure phiala (IV BC)

Скифос от Стрелча

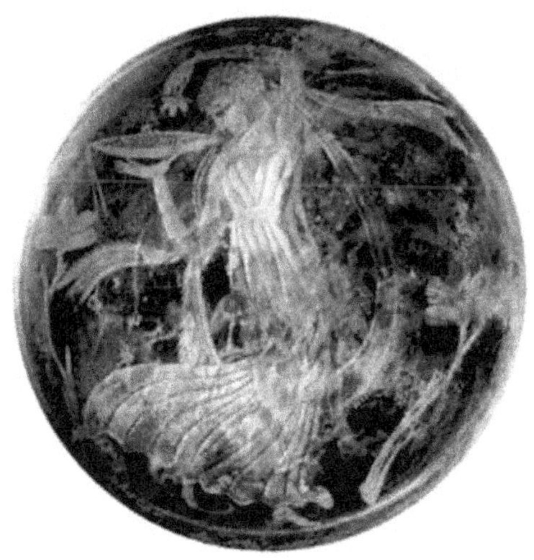

USED ABBREVIATIONS

AJA   – Amnerican Journal of Ancient History.

DK   – **Diels H.-Kranz, W.** 1951-1952. *Fragmente der Vorsokratiker*, sixt. ed., Berlin.

DM   – **Nilsson, M.** 1985. *The Dionysiac Mysteries of the Hellenistic and Roman Age*. Skrifter Utgivna av Svenska Institutet i Athen, Lund.

Epigr. Gr.   – Kaibel, G. 1878. *Epigrammata graeca ex lapidibus conlecta*, Berlin.

GGR 3, I 580 – **Nilsson, M.** 1955. *Geschichte der griechische Religion*, Muenich.

F.H.G.   – **Mueller G.** 1841-70. *Fragmenta historicorum graecorum*, Paris.

IG   – *Inscriptiones Graecae*, 1873-

LSAM   – **Sokolowski F.**, 1955. *Lois secrées de l'Asie Mineure*, Paris.

LSJ   – Liddell and Scott, Greek-English Lexicon, 9 th edn.

MMR   – **Broughton, T.** The Magistrates of the Roman Republik 1951-2; Suppl. 1986.

OF   – **Kern O.**, 1922 . *Orphicorum fragmenta*, Berlin.

BILIOGRAPHY

Albinus, L. 2000. *The House of Hades: Studies in Ancient Greek Eschatology.* Studies in Religion 2. Aarhus.

Allen, T. et alii, 1936. *The Homeric Hymns.* Oxford. Repr. Amsterdam 1980.

Aly, W. 1912. "Ursprung und Entwicklung der kretischen Zeusreligion." *Philologus* 71:457–478.

Antonelli, C. 1995. "Dioniso e la religione Minoica." In Πεπραγμένα του Ζ´ Διεθνούς Κρητολογικού Συνεδρίου (Ρέθυμνο, 25 –31 Αυγούστου 1991). Vol. A1: Νέα Χριστιανική Κρήτη 11–14 (1994–1995), ed. Nikolaos E. Papadogiannakis, 25–32. Rethymno.

Athanassakis, A. 2004. *The Homeric Hymns.* Translation, introduction, and notes. 2nd ed. Baltimore, MD and London.

Avagianou, A. 1991. *Sacred Marriage in the Rituals of Greek Religion.* European University Studies XV.54. Bern

Babbitt, F. 1931, 1936. *Plutarch's Moralia.* Vols. 3, 5. Loeb Classical Library. Cambridge.

Barker, E. 2002b. "La toile de Pénélope: A-t-il existé un mythe orphique sur Dionysos et les Titans." *Revue de l'histoire des religions* 219:401–433.

Boehringer, D. 2001. *Heroenkulte in Griechenland von der geometrischen bis zur klassischen Zeit.* Klio Beihefte 3. Berlin.

Böhme, R. 1992. Der Lykomide im Homer. *Zeitschrift für Papyrologie und Epigraphik* 94:51–57.

Boteva D., 1997, *St. Athanase d'Etropolé, Sabazios et l'oracle de Dionysos,* Dialogues d'histoire ancienne, 3, 287-298.

Bremmer, J. 1984. The Early Greek Concept of the Soul. Princeton University Press, 1983.

Bremmer, J. 1984. "Greek Maenadism Reconsidered." *Zeitschrift für Papyrologie und Epigraphik* 55:267–286.

Bremmer, J. 2004. "Ritual." In *Religions of the Ancient World: A Guide,* ed. Sarah Iles Johnston, 32–44. Cambridge.

Bremmer, J. 2014. *Initiation into the Mysteries of the Ancient World*, Berlin-Boston.

Brown, A. 1998. "From the Golden Age to the Isles of the Blest." *Mnemosyne* 51:385–410.

Burkert, W.1997 Orphism and Bacchic Mysteries: New Evidence and Old Problems of Interpretation." In *Protocol of the 28th Colloquy of the Center for Hermeneutical Studies in Hellenistic and Modern Culture*, ed. Wilhelm Wuellner, 1–8. Berkeley, CA. (= 2006. In *Walter Burkert Kleine Schriften III: Mystica, Orphica, Pythagorica*. Hypomnemata Supplement-Reihe 2.3, ed. Fritz Graf, 37–46. Göttingen.

Burkert, W. 1985. *Homo Necans. The Anthropology of Ancient Greek Sacrificial Ritual and Myth*, Berkeley: University of California Press, 1983.

Burkert, W. 1985. *Greek Religion*. Trans. John Raffan. Cambridge.

Burkert, W. 1987. *Ancient Mystery Cults*. Cambridge.

Burkert, W. 1993. "Bacchic Teletai in the Hellenistic Age." In *Masks of Dionysus*, ed. Thomas H. Carpenter and Christopher A. Faraone, 259–275. Myth and Poetics. Ithaca, NY. (=Burkert, Walter 2006. In *Walter Burkert Kleine Schriften III: Mystica, Orphica, Pythagorica*. Hypomnemata Supplement-Reihe 2.3, ed. Fritz Graf, 120–136. Göttingen.)

Burkert, Walter, 1994b. "Orpheus, Dionysos und die Euneiden in Athen: Das Zeugnis von Euripides' *Hypsipyle*." In *Orchestra: Drama, Mythos, Bühne*, ed. Anton F. H. Bierl and Peter Möllendorff, with Sabine Vogt, 44–49. Stuttgart and Leipzig. (= 2006. In *Walter Burkert Kleine Schriften III: Mystica, Orphica, Pythagorica*. Hypomnemata Supplement-Reihe 2.3, ed. Fritz Graf, 112–119. Göttingen.)

Burkert, W. 1995. "Greek Poleis and Civic Cults: Some Further Thoughts." In *Studies in the Ancient Greek Polis: Papers from the Copenhagen Polis Centre 2*. Historia Einzelschriften 95, ed. Mogens H. Hansen and Kurt Raaflaub, 201–210. Stuttgart.

Burkert, W. 2001a. "The Formation of Greek Religion at the Close of the Dark Ages." In *Walter Burkert Kleine Schriften I: Homerica*. Hypomnemata Supplement-Reihe 2.1, ed. Christoph Riedweg et al., 13–29. Göttingen.

Burkert, W. 2005b. "Signs, Commands, and Knowledge: Ancient Divination between Enigma and Epiphany." In *Mantike: Studies in Ancient Divination*. Religions in the Graeco-Roman World 155, ed. Sarah Iles Johnston and Peter T. Struck, 29–49. Leiden.

Burkert W. 2011: Dionysos - "different" im Wandel der Zeiten. Eine Skizze. – In: Schlesier, R. (ed.) A Different God. Dionysos and Ancient Polytheism. Berlin, 2011, 15-22.

Carpenter, Th. 1993. *On the Beardless Dionysus.* In *Masks of Dionysus*, ed. Thomas H. Carpenter and Christopher A. Faraone, 185–206. Myth and Poetics. Ithaca, NY.

Carpenter, Th. and Faraone, Ch., eds. 1993. *Masks of Dionysus.* Myth and Poetics. Ithaca, NY.

Chantraine, P. 1980. *Dictionnaire étymologique de la langue grecque: Histoire des mots.* Paris.

Chirassi C. 1991. Le Dionysos oraculaire. *Kernos* 4:205–217.

Cole, S. 1980. *New Evidence for the Mysteries of Dionysus. Greek, Roman, and Byzantine Studies* 21:223–238.

Cole, S. 2003. *Landscapes of Dionysos* ed. 2003. *Greek Mysteries: The Archaeology and Ritual of Ancient Greek Secret Cults.* London.ysian Fields." In *Greek Mysteries: The Archaeology and Ritual of Ancient Greek Secret Cults*, ed. Michael B. Cosmopoulos, 193–217. London and New York.

Cozzoli, A. 2001. *Euripide, Cretesi: Introduzione, testimonianze, testo critico, traduzione e commento.* Testi e Commenti 15. Pisa and Rome.

Daraki, M. 1997. Ὁ Διόνυσος καὶ ἡ θεὰ Γῆ. Athens.

De Heer, C. 1969. *Μάκαρ, εὐδαίμων, ὄλβιος, εὐτυχής: A Study of the Semantic Field Denoting Happiness in Ancient Greek to the End of the 5th Century B.C.* Amsterdam.

De Polignac, Fr. 1996. "Entre les dieux et les morts: Statut individuel et rites collectifs dans la cité archaïque." In *The Role of Religion in the Early Greek Polis: Proceedings of the Third International Seminar on Ancient Greek Cult, organized by the Swedish Institute at Athens, 16–18 October 1992.* Skrifter Utgivna av Svenska Institutet i Athen 8.14, ed. Robin Hägg, 31–40. Stockholm.

Detienne, M. 1979. *Dionysos Slain.* Trans. Mireille Muellner and Leonard Muellner. Baltimore.

Detienne, M. 1989. *Dionysos at Large.* Trans. Arthur Goldhammer. Cambridge.

Dimitrov K. 2012. The Cult of Dionyssos in Seuthopolis. – Orpheus19, 23-48.

Dodds, E. 1951. *The Greeks and the Irrational.* Sather Classical Lectures 25. Berkeley, CA.

Dodds, E. 1960. *Euripides. Bacchae* . Edited with introduction and commentary. Oxford.

Dover, K. 1997. *Aristophanes. Frogs.* Abridged from the 1993 edition. Oxford.

Farnell, L. 1995. *Greek Hero Cults and Ideas of Immortality: The Gifford Lectures Delivered in the University of St. Andrewes in the Year 1920.* Chicago. Orig. pub. Oxford, 1921.

Farnell, L. 2004. *The Cults of the Greek States.* 5 vols. Chicago. Orig. pub. Oxford, 1896–1909.

Filow, B. 1937/38. *Thrakisch-mykenische Beziehungen.* - RIEB, 3, 1-2, 1-7, 1937/38.

Fol, Al. 2004. *Die thrakische Orphik oder zwei Wege zur Unsterblichkeit. Die Thraker: Das goldene Reich des Orpheus, 23. Juli bis 28. November 2004,* 177–186. Bonn.

Fol, Al. 2004, Orphica Magica, Sofia.

Graf, Fr. 1980. *Milch, Honig und Wein: Zum Verständnis der Libation im griechischen Ritual. Perennitas: Studi in onore di Angelo Brelich promossi dalla Cattedra di Religioni del mondo classico dell'Università degli Studi di Roma,* 209–221. Rome.

Guthrie, W, 1993. *Orpheus and Greek Religion: A Study of the Orphic Movement.* Princeton.

Guthrie, W, 1950. *The Greeks and Their Gods.* Beacon Press, Boston.

Halm-Tisserant, M. 2004. *Le sparagmos, un rite de magie fécondant. Kernos* 17:119–142.

Henrichs, Al. 1978. *Greek Maenadism from Olympias to Messalina. Harvard Studies in Classical Philology* 82:121–160.

Henrichs, Al. 1984a. "Loss of Self, Suffering, Violence: The Modern View of Dionysos from Nietzsche to Girard." *Harvard Studies in Classical Philology* 101:207–266.

Henrichs, Al. 1984b. "Male Intruders Among the Maenads: The So-Called Male Celebrant." In *MNEMAI: Classical Studies in Memory of Karl K. Hulley,* ed. Harold D. Evjen, 69–91. Chico.

Henrichs, Al. 1990. "Between Country and City: Cultic Dimensions of Dionysus in Athens and Attica." In *Cabinet of the Muses: Essays on Classical and Comparative Literature in Honor of Thomas G. Rosenmeyer*, ed. Mark Griffith and Donald J. Mastronarde, 257–277. Atlanta.

Henrichs, Al. 1993a. "'He Has a God in Him': Human and Divine in the Modern Perception of Dionysus." In *Masks of Dionysus*, ed. Thomas H. Carpenter and Christopher A. Faraone, 13–43. Myth and Poetics. Ithaca.

Henrichs, Al. 1993b. "Gods in Action: The Poetics of Divine Performance in the Hymns of Callimachus." In *Callimachus: Proceedings of the Groningen Workshops on Hellenistic Poetry*. Hellenistica Groningana I, ed. M. Annette Harder, Remco F. Regtuit, and Gerry C. Wakker, 127–147. Groningen.

Henrichs, Al. 1995. Why Should I Dance?: Choral Self-Referentiality in Greek Tragedy. *Arion* 3:56–111.

Henrichs, Al. 1998. "Dromena und Legomena: Zum rituellen Selbstverständnis der Griechen." In *Ansichten griechischer Rituale: Geburstags-Symposium für Walter Burkert, Castelen bei Basel 15. bis 18. März 1996*, ed. Fritz Graf, 33–71. Stuttgart and Leipzig.

Henrichs, Al. 2000. *Drama and Dromena: Bloodshed, Violence, and Sacrificial Metaphor in Euripides. Harvard Studies in Classical Philology* 100:173–188.

Henrichs, Al. 2003a. *Hieroi Logoi and Hierai Bibloi: The (Un)written Margins of the Sacred in Ancient Greece. Harvard Studies in Classical Philology* 88:205–240.

Henrichs, Al. 2003b. *Writing Religion: Inscribed Texts, Ritual Authority, and the Religious Discourse of the Polis*. In *Written Texts and the Rise of Literate Culture in Ancient Greece*, ed. Harvey Yunis, 38–58. Cambridge and New York.

Henrichs, Al. 2004a. *Sacred Texts and Canonicity: Greece*. In *Religions of the Ancient World: A Guide*, ed. Sarah Iles Johnston, 633–635. Cambridge.

Henrichs, Al. 2004b. Let the Good Prevail': *Perversions of the Ritual Process in Greek Tragedy*. In *Greek Ritual Poetics*. Center for Hellenic Studies, Hellenic Studies Series 3, ed. Dimitrios Yatromanolakis and Panagiotis Roilos, 189–198. Washington, and Cambridge.

Isaac B., 1986. *The Greek Settlements in Thrace until the Macedonian Conquest*. Leiden, E.J. Brill,

Jaccottet A., 2003. *Choisir Dionysos. Les associations dionysiaques ou la face cachée du dionysisme. Vol. I: Text; II: Documents.* Zürich: Akanthus

Jaeger W., 1936. *The Theology of the Early Greek Philosophers,* The Gifford Lectures, Oxford University Press.

Kirk G., 1970. *Myth Its Meaning and Functions in Ancient and Other Cultures.* Cambridge: University Press and California: University Press.

Kakouri K., 1965. *Dionysiaka,* Eng. trans. Aspects of the Popular Thracian Worship of To-day, Athens, G.C. Eleftheroudakis.

Lada-Richards, Is. 1999. *Initiating* Ladianou, Katerina. 2005. "The Poetics of *Choreia*: Imitation and Dance in the *Anacreonteia.*" *Quaderni Urbinati di Cultura Classica* 80:47–58.*Dionysus: Ritual and Theatre in Aristophanes' Frogs.* Oxford.

LIMC. 1981–1997. *Lexicon Iconographicum Mythologiae Classicae,* ed. John Boardman et al. Zürich.**Marazov I.** 2000, Thracians and Wine, Sofia.

McDonald, M. 1978. *Terms for Happiness in Euripides.* Hypomnemata 54. Göttingen.

Nilsson, M. 1950. *The Minoan-Mycenaean Religion and its Survival in Greek Religion.* 2nd rev. ed. Skrifter Utgivna av Kungl: Humanistiska Vetenskapssamfundet i Lund 9. Lund.

Nilsson, M. 1985. *The Dionysiac Mysteries of the Hellenistic and Roman Age.* Skrifter Utgivna av Svenska Institutet i Athen 8.5. Lund 1957. Repr. Salem.

Nock, A. 1972. *Essays on Religion and the Ancient World,* ed. Z. Stewart, Oxford.

Obbink, D. 1993. "Dionysus Poured Out: Ancient and Modern Theories of Sacrifice and Cultural Formation." In *Masks of Dionysus,* ed. Thomas H. Carpenter and Christopher A. Faraone, 65–86. Myth and Poetics. Ithaca.

Parker, R. 1983. *Miasma: Pollution and Purification in Early Greek Religion.* Oxford.

Parker, R. 1991. "The *Hymn to Demeter* and the *Homeric Hymns.*" *Greece & Rome* 38:1–17.

Parker, R. 1995. "Early Orphism." In *The Greek World,* ed. Anton Powell, 483–510. London.

Parker, R. 1996. *Athenian Religion: A History*. Oxford.

Parker, R. 2000a. *Greek States and Greek Oracles*. In *Oxford Readings in Greek Religion*, ed. Richard Buxton, 76–108. Oxford.

Parker, R. 2000b. *Heiliges Wort und Heilige Schrift bei den Griechen: Hieroi Logoi und verwandte Erscheinungen."* Bryn Mawr Classical Review 2000.

Parker, R. 2005. *Polytheism and Society in Ancient Athens*. Oxford.

Paton, Sara. 2004. "The Villa Dionysos at Knossos: Recent Work." In *Creta romana e protobizantina: Atti del congresso internazionale organizzato dalla Scuola Archeologica Italiana di Atene (Iraklion, 23–30 settembre 2000)*, ed. Antonino Di Vita, Monica Livadioti, and Ilaria Simiakaki, vol. 2:281–285. Padua.

Perdrizet, P. 1910. *Cultes et mythes du Pangée*. Paris-Nancy, 1910.

Picard, Ch. 1946. "La triade Zeus-Héra-Dionysos dans l'Orient hellénique d'après les nouveaux fragments d'Alcée." *Bulletin de Correspondance Hellénique* 70:455–473.

Peek, W.1955. *Griechische Vers-Inschriften I: Grab-Epigramme* . Berlin

Piérart, M. 1996. *La mort de Dionysos à Argos*. In *The Role of Religion in the Early Greek Polis: Proceedings of the Third International Seminar on Ancient Greek Cult, organized by the Swedish Institute at Athens, 16–18 October 1992*. Skrifter Utgivna av Svenska Institutet i Athen 8.14, ed. Robin Hägg, 141–151. Stockholm.

Preller-Robert. 1894.*Griechische Mythologie*, I, Berlin, Weidmann.

Rapp, A. 1882. *Die Beziehungen des Dionysosuskultes zu Thrakien und Kleinasien*, Stuttgart, 1882

Rhode, E. 1987. *Psyche: The Cult of Souls and Belief in Immortality Among the Ancient Greeks*. Trans. W. B. Hillis. London 1925. Repr. Chicago.

Rudhardt, J. 2002. *Les deux mères de Dionysos, Perséphone et Sémélé, dans les Hymnes orphiques. Revue de l'histoire des religions* 219:483–501.

Seaford, R. 1981. "Dionysiac Drama and the Dionysiac Mysteries." *Classical Quarterly* 31:252–275.

Seaford, R. 1986. *Immortality, Salvation, and the Elements. Harvard Studies in Classical Philology* 90:1–26.

Seaford, R. 1993. *Dionysus as Destroyer of the Household: Homer, Tragedy, and the Polis*. In *Masks of Dionysus*, ed. Thomas H. Carpenter and Christopher A. Faraone, 115–146. Myth and Poetics. Ithaca, NY.

Seaford, R. 1994. *Sophokles and the Mysteries. Hermes* 122:275–288.

Seaford, R. 1996. *Euripides. Bacchae* . With an introduction, translation and commentary. Warminster.

Seaford, R. 2006. *Dionysos: Gods and Heroes of the Ancient World*. London and New York.

Snodgrass, A. 2000. "The Archaeology of the Hero." In *Oxford Readings in Greek Religion*, ed. Richard Buxton, 180–190. Oxford.

Sokolowski, Fr. 1962. *Lois sacrées de cités grecques. Supplément* . École française d'Athènes. Travaux et mémoires des anciens membres étrangers de l'École et de divers savants 11. Paris.

Tacheva-Hitova M. 1983. *Eastern Cults in Moesia Inferior and Thracia (5th Century BC – 4th Century AD)*. Leiden: E. J. Brill.

Usener, H. 1896. *Götternamen: Versuch einer Lehre von der Religiösen Begriffsbildung*, Bonn.

Ustinova, Y. 2002 *Either a Daimon, or a Hero, or Perhaps a God: Mythical Residents of Subterranean Chambers*, Kernos 15, 267-288, 2002.

West M., 1983. The Orphik Poems, Oxford.

Богданов, Б. 2016. *Орфей и древната митология на Балканите*, София .

Василева, М. 2005. *Цар Мидас между Европа и Азия*, София

Вълчинова, Г. , 2000, *Лудост и mania: два погледа към отклонението от нормалното в древните и традиционните култури*, Seminarium Thracicum, Sofia, 173-188.

Венедиков, Ив. 1983. *Медното гумно на прабългарите*, София.

Гандева, Р. 1983. *Тракийски мотиви в римската литература*, София.

Гочева, З. 2008. *Марон – жрец на кикdoните или жрец на Аполон*, Societas classsica, 259-

Данов, Х. 1968. *Древна Тракия. Изследвания върху историята на българските земи, Северна Добруджа, Източна и Егейска Тракия от края на IX до края на III век пр. н.е.*, София.

Дечев, Д. 1945, *Тракийският херос като бог ловец,* Списание на БАН, т. LXX, кл. Историко-филологически, XXXIII,197-198.

Дечев, Д. 1952, *Една семейна триада в религията на траките,* Известия на археологическия институт, т. XVIII.

Йорданова, М. 2013, *HAGNA THYMATA. Антропологични аспекти на безкръвната орфическа жертва,* Studia Classica Serdicensia II, Университетско издателство "Св. Климент Охридски" София, 123-134.

Лазова, Ц. 2001, *Хипербореите: обред и повествование,* София.

Lozanova, V. 1995, *The Mysteries of the Thracian Kotytia.* София, 1995.

Маразов, Ив. 1992, *Мит, ритуал и изкуство у траките,* София.

Маразов, Ив. 1994, *Митология на траките,* София.

Михайлов, Г. 1972, *Траките,* София.

Попов, Д. 1995, *Богът с многото имена,* София.

Райчевски, С., Фол, В. 1993, *Кукерът без маска,* София.

Фол, Ал. 1975, *Тракия и Балканите през ранноелинистическата епоха,* София.

Фол, Ал.1989, *Главното светилище на Дионис,* Култура, 2, 71-80.

Фол Ал. 1989, *Тракия и Македония през VI-V в. пр. н.е в Еврипидовите „Вакханки",* Култура, 5, 51-56.

Фол, Ал. 1986. *Тракийският орфизъм,* София.

Фол, Ал. 1991. *Тракийският Дионис. Книга първа. Загрей,* София.

Фол, Ал. 1994. *Тракийският Дионис. Книга втора: Сабазий.* София.

Фол, Ал. 2002.*Тракийският Дионис. Книга трета.* Назоваване и вяра. София.

Тачева, М. 1982: История на източните култове в Долна Мизия и Тракия /Vв. пр. Хр. - IV в./, София, 1982 = M. Tacheva-Hitova. Eastern Cults in Moesia Inferior and Thracia (5th Century BC – 4th Century AD). Leiden: E. J. Brill (1983).

Mihaela Jordanova

MAENADS – EARLY DIONYSIAC RITES

First edition

Desktop publishing:
www.Mind-Print.com

Sofia
2017